IMPACT

THE ARMY AIR FORCES' CONFIDENTIAL PICTURE HISTORY OF WORLD WAR II

*Declassified and now published
for the general public for the first time
with fourteen new retrospective essays
by World War II leaders and journalists*

ONWARD TOWARD TOKYO

James Parton, Consulting Editor

Sponsored by
THE AIR FORCE HISTORICAL FOUNDATION

Published by
NATIONAL HISTORICAL SOCIETY, HARRISBURG, PA.

Cover: 5th Air Force C-47s drop a paratroop battalion at Nadzab, New Guinea (*Impact,* October 1943)

Tactical Air Power: Cutting The Enemy's Arms And Legs

Essays by

General Jacob L. Devers, USA (Ret.)
and
Lieutenant General Elwood R. Quesada, USAF (Ret.)

★1★
THE GROUND SIDE

by General Jacob L. Devers, USA (Ret.)

About the author: *A West Pointer, Class of 1909, Jacob L. Devers was "one hundred per cent the military professional in the finest sense of the term," as Henry Cabot Lodge Jr. described him in a Senate tribute upon his retirement in 1949 as Chief, Army Field Forces, "which is the fighting end of the Army."*

In the intervening forty years Devers served in so many posts that only the high spots can be included here. Sent abroad in World War I too late for any fighting, he spent a fruitful year in France and Germany, returning to the slow climb to high command—Chief of Armored Force, 1941; Commanding General, European Theater of Operations, 1943; Deputy Supreme Allied Commander, Mediterranean, 1944, under Field Marshal Sir Maitland Wilson. In August of that year he commanded "Operation Dragoon," the invasion of southern France, which swiftly captured the vital port of Marseilles and swept north to link with Eisenhower's forces advancing from Normandy.

For the remaining bitter nine months of battle, Ike worked through three commanders—Montgomery, in command of the Northern Group of Armies; Bradley, in command of the Central Group; and Devers in command of the Southern. The last, officially designated the Sixth Army Group, consisted of the Seventh U. S. Army and the First French Army. The 700,000 men under Devers, working smoothly with Air Force Tactical support, moved through the Vosges mountains around the north of Switzerland to capture all of Austria and reach Innsbruck by May 1945. Especially gratifying was the liberation along the way of the remaining prisoners at notorious Dachau.

On May 6, 1945, he took the unconditional surrender of Army Group G, comprising all German forces in Austria—slightly less than one million men, including Goering, Kesselring and Von Runstedt.

In his remarks to the Senate, Lodge commented: "I believe it was the historian Herodotus who said, 'I would rather be in the general's tent the night before the battle than to hear his speech the day after the victory.' There were never any speeches after victories, but those who were in General Devers's tent the night before the battle can testify that being there was a reassuring experience."

—J.P.

Since 1939 it has been clear to me that the tactical airplane and the tank are natural partners. The Germans demonstrated that when they moved so quickly into Poland and then into France. Their tanks were most successful when they had air superiority. The tank and the tactical airplane work best when they work together.

As an artilleryman and a tank man, I was intensely interested in new ideas, new weapons and mobility. Well before our involvement in World War II it became eminently clear to me that the airplane, along with the tank, was a valuable weapon. Initially it was a single-engine plane, assigned for my personal use as Chief of the Armored Force for frequent travel on short notice, that taught me to respect the mobility offered by air travel. I was not a pilot, but one of my aides was an excellent flyer.

In the summer before Pearl Harbor when we held our big war games—the Louisiana maneuvers—I observed the way each side coordinated the use of airplanes with the use of tanks and became convinced of the need for a tactical air force to work with ground troops. Air doctrine has gradually evolved a clear distinction between strategic and tactical operations. *Strategic* air hits enemy targets beyond the theater of contending armies and navies, cutting down war production and reducing the morale of the homeland and the will of its leaders. *Tactical* air gives close support to ground and naval forces. Both strategic and tactical often combine to provide the air superiority always essential to military success.

My appreciation of air warfare and the way it aids, complements and supplements tanks and artillery in ground fighting increased in late 1942, when General Frank M. Andrews flew me around North Africa to the United States air bases there.

Thus, in May 1943, when Army Chief of Staff General George C. Marshall sent me to England to become senior American commander of the European Theater, I was well-informed on Air Force matters. That was fortunate, because, along with the Army and Navy components, I had jurisdiction over the Army Air Force elements in that theater.

The Eighth Air Force in England was commanded by Ira Eaker, who had a fighter command and a bomber command. He and I were on the same wavelength and got along fine. He had enormous problems—whole groups of his men and airplanes had been transferred to North Africa, the buildup in England was slower than promised and his strategic air war against Germany was being delayed.

I had a dual role at that time: to help the Eighth Air Force in every way I would, and also to build up men and supplies for the Normandy invasion. As Commander of the European Theater I could help, for I was working with the top British people from Prime Minister Winston Churchill and the Chiefs of Staff on down, including the RAF.

One of Eaker's jobs was to build or modify 120 airfields, in itself an enormous task. Meantime, the Eighth Air Force had knotty problems such as the acquisition of more bomber groups, replacement crews, long-range fighters for escort and a steady supply of hundreds of necessary items, the urgent need for better weather forecasting over England and the Continent, and, of vital importance, Eaker's battle for daylight bombing. Because of my position and my strong belief in the importance of air warfare, I was able to assist him in some of these matters.

In the fall of 1943, General Eisenhower was named Supreme Commander for the planned invasion of Nazi-occupied Europe. I was sent to North Africa to replace him and he moved to England, bringing his air team with him—General Carl Spaatz and General James Doolittle. Eaker moved to Italy as Commander in Chief of the Mediterranean Allied Air Force (MAAF) so once again he and I were working as a team. We were both under the direction of Field Marshal Henry "Jumbo" Wilson, and we all had our headquarters in the palace of the former King of Naples at Caserta, twelve miles north of Naples. Wilson was a fine man. I thought him the best of all British generals.

Italy presented a wholly different situation. It was broader in scope than the operation in England and more far-flung. The Allies were fighting a very tough ground war against an experienced, well-equipped German army under Field Marshal Alfred Kesselring, a capable and battle-wise commander. The mountain terrain favored the defenders and they were well dug in, usually on hillsides above us. It was a foot-slogging war which our troops, and the British and French, had to fight foot by foot through mountainous country.

On the air side, Ira Eaker had two U. S. Air Forces: the Fifteenth was strategic, under Major General Nathan F. Twining. The Twelfth was tactical, under Major General John Cannon. Eaker's MAAF also had the British Desert and Balkan Air Forces and the Coastal Air Forces, plus the French squadrons. MAAF had a real international flavor, with pilots from the United States, Britain, France, Poland, Yugoslavia and Italy. They flew some thirty different types of aircraft.

The Fifteenth reached out into Germany, Austria, Czechoslovakia and Rumania to bomb strategic targets in a partnership with the U. S. Eighth Air Force in England. The Twelfth performed a tactical role of the greatest importance in support of my operations through southern France. I have an especially warm spot in my heart for the Twelfth Air Force.

I should say a word about Anzio, which was conceived and planned before Eaker and I arrived in Italy and took place shortly after we got there. On D-Day, January 22, our troops went ashore and rapidly pushed seven miles inland. The beach area was never free of German shelling, as Eaker and I discovered when we landed on the improvised air strip on D-Day and shells began falling around us. A jeep raced up and the driver shouted, "For God's sake, get out of there and into this," and he hurried us off. A nearby hospital was hit, I remember, and some nurses and many patients were killed.

The Germans saw Anzio correctly as an Allied effort to link up Anzio with the U. S. Fifth and British Eighth Armies and move on to Rome. Kesselring hurriedly withdrew troops from both ends of his line across Italy and even brought reinforcements from southern France and the Balkans. On the thirty-five-mile Anzio front the enemy soon had ten divisions against our five. Fifth Army could not move forward. The valiant action of our artillery in the beach area, combined with the heroic work of the Twelfth Air Force, beat off several strong German counterattacks. While the Germans could not win, neither could we, and a stalemate followed. But without strong tactical air power on our side the struggle at Anzio would have been even more difficult than it was.

Other disappointments that spring were the two bombing attacks on the Abbey atop Monte Cassino and the town at its base—a plan that Field Marshal Wilson, Eaker and I had strongly resisted. But the ground commander who was to lead the troops there insisted that Cassino be bombed, and he got his way.

The early weeks of 1944 were not a happy time for us in Italy. The war plan called for the Allied armies to move north, take Rome and sweep the Germans into northern Italy. But neither the British nor the American army could break out. To overcome this stalemate, and to bolster Cassino and Anzio, we planned a tactical air operation known as "Strangle," which proved to be a triumphant success.

The objective was to carry out the classical role of a tactical air force: to isolate the battlefield by cutting off men and supplies to Kesselring. His eighteen German divisions needed 4,000 tons of supplies every day. During an Allied offensive they needed 5,000 tons. We knew they could not operate if we could cut off supplies coming down the peninsula from northern Italy and from Germany.

Our tactical aircraft bombed and strafed railroad lines, trains, marshaling yards, repair facilities, bridges, tunnels, viaducts and, later, highways used by trucks. We knew that cuts in rail lines could be repaired fairly quickly (unless there were too many of them), but a knocked-out bridge or viaduct or a tunnel blocked at each end, would take days or weeks to repair.

"Strangle" began on March 19 and continued until about May 13. The Twelfth Air Force threw everything it had into the fight. Many kinds of MAAF planes were used: fighters, fighter-bombers, medium bombers, night-flying Wellingtons, plus B-24s and B-17s from the Fifteenth Air Force. Pilots from Coastal Command and the Desert Air Force joined in. More than 10,000 sorties were flown the first week.

The accuracy of bombing bridges improved steadily until almost all important bridges were knocked out. Attacks on viaducts that carried trains high over narrow valleys were highly successful. To rebuild such structures was difficult, and when they were rebuilt they were soon struck again. Marshaling yards with their hundreds of loaded freight cars were a prize target, especially the big yards at Rome.

The Germans also sent supplies down the coast by ship. As rail traffic diminished, coastal shipping became more important. Our air forces attacked every ship they could find, and a high proportion were sunk. Coastal ports were attacked day and night.

There was little or no opposition from the Luftwaffe. Not only were German planes shot down when they appeared, but their airfields were bombed repeatedly. B-17s and B-24s of the Fifteenth Air Force destroyed a group of fields in the north Adriatic area where enemy fighters were concentrated. We had complete air superiority, a decisive factor.

With rail lines cut in so many places that trains were almost entirely stopped, Kesselring had to rely on truck traffic. Truck drivers, many of whom were Italian, refused to drive in the day time, knowing it meant almost certain strafing and probably death. At night they were forced to use secondary roads, which slowed them down. By the end of April only a trickle of the great tonnage the Germans needed was getting through to the front lines.

In the eight weeks of "Strangle," MAAF pilots flew some 65,000 sorties, or an average of 1,350 per day—a most impressive record. The attacks were simultaneous over the entire German transportation system. And they were continuous, day after day. The success of this campaign is more remarkable considering the fact that flying weather was poor almost half the time.

The payoff came on May 11. Ground troops began their offensive. Thanks to the air attacks, the enemy was short of almost everything they needed. Anzio forces attacked out of the beachhead and linked up with the Fifth Army. The Fifth and Eighth Armies moved ahead. The Gustav Line collapsed. Rome was taken—and Kesselring's forces moved back into central Italy, and then further north.

During the German retreat, MAAF's tactical air forces kept up their onslaught. On May 24 alone, more than 3,200 sorties were flown against roads, railroads, supplies, trucks and tanks. Medium bombers and fighter-bombers created roadblocks in critical locations; then, as traffic piled up, our fighters moved in to destroy everything on the roads below. More than 3,000 vehicles were wiped out in June. Only a large and experienced air force could have carried out such an impressive task.

The best testimony of tactical air's results came to us from German prisoners. What one Luftwaffe ground-crew sergeant told interviewers is typical: "Our withdrawals were always a fearful shambles. We traveled only at night and rested in the daytime. At four-thirty in the morning we had to start taking cover, because your fighters appeared then. We were never safe from bombing in the daytime. Everything moving on the roads was shot up."

The Allied advance in May and June paved the way for our next big effort—the invasion of southern France on August 15. It turned out to be the most successful of all the army-navy-air force landings in the Mediterranean. Our planning was based on experiences that began in North Africa and continued at Pantelleria, Sicily, southern Italy, Anzio and Elba. It became a textbook demonstration of how to carry out landing operations.

I was enthusiastic about this campaign and took an active part in the detailed planning. I was to command two armies that were to become the 6th Army Group: the American Seventh under Lieutenant General Alexander M. Patch and the First French under General Jean de Lattre de Tassigny.

We hoped to accomplish at least three objectives—to take the two big ports of Marseilles and Toulon on the south coast, to sweep the Germans out of south and central France, and then to take our places on the southern end of a great line of Allied armies stretching from the English Channel to Switzerland.

I knew that taking the ports and getting them ready to serve American supply ships was of the greatest importance, and I had talked with both General Marshall and Eisenhower about it. One of the Allies' greatest needs was ports. The enemy was fighting tenaciously to hold the English Channel ports and then were wrecking them before surrendering. Not only were the two southern ports large and serviceable, they were actually closer to large areas of France and Germany than were the northern ports. In the Battle of the Bulge, sixty per cent of all Allied supplies came through Marseilles and Toulon.

The tactical air force began softening up targets in southern France a month or more before our invasion. They hit communication lines so enemy troops could not move about freely. They helped to carry out a cover plan to make the enemy think we would be attacking either over near Spain or in the corner near Italy.

Our intelligence estimated the Germans had 450 big guns along the south coast and 1,700 lighter guns. Those were formidable numbers, and tactical air forces were assigned to knock them out. Big navy guns had been installed to protect the harbors at Marseilles and Toulon, and heavy bombers from the Fifteenth Air Force were sent in to bomb them. German airfields were also attacked and kept out of action.

D-Day, August 15, was the payoff for our careful planning and preliminary air attacks. Shortly after daylight, as TAC fighters provided air cover, pathfinder groups parachuted into LeMuy, about twenty miles behind the beaches. They had electronic equipment to guide C-47 pilots who would soon be bringing in more than five thousand British and American paratroopers despite cloudy weather and ground haze. Four hours later forty more C-47s towing gliders brought in more airborne troops.

Early that morning MAAF flew 900 sorties against coastal guns and beach obstacles. Despite the ground fog their bombing was extraordinarily accurate. Then the Navy sent its mine sweepers close to the beaches, followed by warships that shot thousands of projectiles into beach defenses.

Before 0800 the armada of troop ships began arriving from half a dozen Italian and North African ports. We had almost complete air superiority and no ships were lost.

Thanks to naval and air bombardment, ground troops had an easy time going ashore, except at one beach where German gunners continued to be active for a short time. General Patch told me he gave the Air Force credit for preventing many ground force casualties.

I watched the invasion on D-Day from the air, riding on a jump seat behind the pilot of a P-38, with Ira Eaker flying alongside us in his P-51. We flew over LeMuy to see where the paratroops had landed and then flew up the Rhone Valley to get a quick look at what was ahead. We were low and could see scores of trucks, tanks and other vehicles destroyed by air attacks.

Then Eaker and I joined the naval commander on his flagship. As we were boarding, a German JU-88 came out of the clouds and dropped butterfly bombs on the ship. We were not hit, but some of our aides were wounded. The official count that day indicated that the Germans flew about 60 sorties all told. Some observers saw no enemy planes or caught fleeting glimpses of only one or two. MAAF flew more than 4,200 sorties, so there was not much chance for a German pilot to get in. Having air support like that gave a great boost to ground force morale, and certainly to mine.

In the afternoon we watched more C-47s fly over with loads of paratroopers, and there were also more glider missions. It gave us added confidence to know that almost all of the 9,000 paratroopers had landed safely and that we had such a strong force of tough men out there behind the beaches.

Landings from troop ships went on all day and into the evening. By late afternoon the beaches had been linked up and our advance units had pushed out to join up with airborne troops.

That landing was a perfect demonstration of the way an invasion could be carried out. I stood on the deck of the flagship. Overhead the air was literally filled with our planes, including carrier-based aircraft from both Navies; below them, our men were moving safely ashore. This D-Day was a great triumph for all of us.

One reason ground and air cooperation went smoothly was because of the efficient work of my air officer, Brigadier General Gordon Saville. He had been operations officer of the Twelfth Air Force, and his background could not have been better. He remained at my side for the rest of the war.

We had feared that Marseilles and Toulon would be strongly defended and that it might take us until D + 40 to capture them. But the air attacks, along with the fighting of the French forces and Patch's Seventh Army, were so successful that both ports surrendered on D + 3. Conquering those ports was indeed a triumph and of the greatest importance.

By the end of the first week, enemy troops had stopped moving south as possible reinforcements and had turned north to join the many thousands of Germans rushing toward the Rhine. Their retreat turned into a rout to escape being caught between us and Patton's army, which was moving toward Germany. Their escape was slowed because our Air Force had knocked out so many bridges and they could not use the blocked railroads.

Our tactical air forces had a field day. They shot up everything that moved on the roads, attacking hour after hour through the long days, and often by parachute flares at night.

On September 11, less than a month after the

invasion, our advance units met the American Third Army. Patch moved into a line south of Patton and the French First Army held the southernmost position.

During the invasion of southern France I had frequent meetings with de Lattre, the French commander, and occasionally with de Gaulle. I found that de Gaulle had keen military acumen and we got along well.

The Germans were now fighting with their backs to the Rhine, and their orders from Hitler were not to retreat a foot. They had shorter supply lines. In our southern area the Vosges mountains were very rough country, favoring the enemy.

As the battle line became stabilized the role of the tactical air forces changed. Offensive work of fighters and fighter-bombers went on. There were night operations, attacks by medium bombers, and aerial spotting for our artillery. Aerial reconnaissance was of great importance, as we needed to know what the enemy was doing. Photos were duplicated and distributed to ground commanders who were eager to get them. And always our fighter pilots kept enemy planes off our backs.

In March and April of 1945 the war again became fluid as we moved ahead. Ground commanders depended on their air partners to tell them what was out in front. There were continuous air attacks on bridges, railroads, roads, supply dumps, command posts, airfields and other installations.

In my meetings with Eisenhower and General Omar Bradley, and of course with Patch and de Lattre, we never planned a move without considering what tactical air could do and how it could best be used. We had a true partnership with our air commanders. The flexibility of tactical groups gave us a tremendous advantage. There were thirty or more groups serving Bradley and me. They were moved back and forth along the front. Extra air strength was available wherever and whenever it was needed most.

Tactical air power came into its own in World War II. Without it on our side the war would have dragged on much longer and we would have suffered many more casualties. In each phase of the war in Europe the air battle had to be won first. Tactical and strategic air forces working together shortened the war and made final victory possible.

⋆2⋆
THE AIR SIDE

by Lieutenant General Elwood R. Quesada, USAF (Ret.)

About the author: *"Pete" Quesada, as he was universally known, was most at home in a fighter cockpit, as in the P-38 in England in 1944 at left, but his talents were manifold and he quickly caught the eye of his seniors in the tiny Air Corps when commissioned in 1927.*

Thus, a year later, he became flying aide to General James E. Fechet, Chief of Air Corps, and, after a tour as assistant military attache in Cuba, flying aide to F. Trubee Davison, Assistant Secretary of War for Air. When the "Question Mark" set an endurance record in 1929 with Major (later General) Carl Spaatz in command and Captain (later General) Ira Eaker as pilot, Lieutenant Quesada was co-pilot. In 1933, with four months accumulated leave, Quesada flew Davison and Martin Johnson all over Africa in a Sikorsky amphibian, collecting animals for the New York Museum of Natural History. And when the Air Corps was ordered to fly the mail in the winter of 1933-1934, Pete Quesada, still a Lieutenant, was chief pilot of the New York-Cleveland route.

A variety of other pre-war assignments led to his promotion to Brigadier in 1942 and command of the Twelfth Air Force Fighter Command in North Africa, where he flew many operational missions during the Tunisian, Sicilian, Corsican and Italian campaigns. He continued with the Twelfth until the landings in Italy were well established, then took over the Ninth Fighter Command in England in October 1943.

He established advanced headquarters on the Normandy beachhead on D-Day plus one and helped provide the aerial cover for the landings. As the invasion front expanded, his assignment was redefined as Commanding General of the Ninth Tactical Air Command, which, until D-Day in Europe, worked in close cooperation with the First U. S. Army.

In April 1945 Quesada returned to Washington as Assistant Chief of Air Staff for Intelligence. In 1946 he took command of the Third Air Force at Tampa. A few weeks later, the Third Air Force was redesignated The Tactical Air Command, with Lieutenant General Quesada in command. Several high staff roles kept him in uniform until 1951. Since then, Quesada has enjoyed substantial success in a variety of business enterprises.

—*J.P.*

To describe my attitude toward tactical air power I need to go back a bit. Though I was a young lieutenant at the time, I went through the years when the Air Corps was fighting for what it believed was its rightful role. Leaders like Billy Mitchell, Hap Arnold, Tooey Spaatz and Ira Eaker were dreaming about what air power could do in the next war: destroy strategic targets far behind enemy lines. We resisted the prevailing idea among army commanders that air power was only an extension of artillery.

During the Battle of Britain I was an air attache in London. There I witnessed the incredible feats of the RAF Fighter Command. When the Germans gave up that battle, the RAF had few fighters and pilots left. I thought then, and I still think, that if the Germans had had a real strategic air force they could have knocked England out of the war.

Pre-war, I was commander of a fighter group. After the invasion of North Africa I was sent there and became Deputy Commander of the Northwest African Air Force and Commander of the Twelfth Air Force Fighter Command. Our assignment, in addition to the traditional role of supporting ground troops, was to work with the U. S. and British navies to stop supplies and reinforcements from reaching Field Marshal Erwin Rommel.

Through various means we learned when convoys were being loaded at Italian docks and which routes they were taking to Africa. With this information we could use our medium bombers and our fighter-bombers effectively. Sometimes airplanes sighting a convoy would notify our submarines. Other times, submarines seeing a convoy would notify us to launch our strikes.

Some information came from photo-reconnaissance pilots who took pictures of Italian ports or of convoys leaving Italian ports. But of most value, we were getting intercepts of radio messages from Hitler to Field Marshal Alfred Kesselring in Italy, and also interchanges between Kesselring and Rommel. This important information came to us from "Ultra," the organization in England which broke the German code.

One day, for example, Ultra told us that Rommel was to get much-needed gasoline to be flown over from Italy in 100 JU-52 transport planes. In what was called "the Big Turkey Shoot" our fighter pilots knocked down most of them.

Our tactical airplanes also had the job of defending our seaports at night. German bombers could not attack in the daytime because our defenses would exact prohibitive losses. At night they could sometimes sneak in one or two bombers.

In October 1943 I moved to England and joined the Ninth Air Force. There I had two jobs, commanding the 9th Fighter Command and IX Tactical Air Command. Our primary job was initially to fly escort for the B-17s and B-24s of the Eighth Air Force in their bombing missions over the continent. They needed fighter escort, especially on the deep penetrations.

After the late fall of 1943, the buildup of tactical air units in England proceeded at an incredible pace. The excellent training and equipment of those new fighter groups surprised me. I had no idea that fighter pilots without combat experience could be so effective. They were also ably led by their group and squadron commanders. In some cases, in three or four days after arrival at their air bases they were flying combat missions over the Continent. Our training and supply people at home deserve much credit.

We were the first Tactical Air Force to get P-51s—the Mustangs. They were the ideal escort plane because they could fly further and stay over the target longer than P-47s or P-38s. As it became clear that the Mustangs were the best for escort, many that were originally scheduled for us went instead to the Eighth Air Force. It would have been wrong to do otherwise. I hated to lose them, but it was a logical move.

Two months before the invasion our role changed. We switched to tactical targets in France, going after bridges over the Seine and Loire. If we could knock out the bridges, the Germans would have a tougher time crossing the rivers in either direction. There was a cover plan to make the enemy think the big Allied attack would come at the Pas de Calais. To pretend we were softening up that area, we had to spend a lot of effort there.

We also bombed railroads, marshaling yards and trains. The life of a locomotive was very short, as trains and engines were easy targets for P-47 pilots. Opposition from German fighters in France was very light. But there was always substantial flak to contend with.

In Normandy, I was fortunate to work with General Omar Bradley. Our IX Tactical Air Command teamed up with the First Army, later commanded by General Courtney Hodges. I believe

General Bradley, as the Commander of our invading army, was immeasurably significant, as was, of course, General George Marshall as the Army Chief of Staff. Bradley was a very fine person—objective and broad-minded. It was easy to see why he was selected for his job. I greatly admired his leadership qualities. He also seemed to like me. After we moved to France our headquarters were side by side. I saw him every day and we often took our meals together.

In my command we then had eighteen fighter groups, one or two reconnaissance groups and a couple of night fighter squadrons. It was a powerful force. Later, half of these groups became the XIX Tactical Air Command, which under General O. P. Weyland, supported Patton's Third Army.

One of my first jobs was to develop a new attitude among our pilots. A fighter pilot naturally wants to get a crack at shooting down his share of enemy planes. We had to teach him that air support involved low flying against tanks, even though hazardous. I spent many hours talking with group and squadron commanders, and also with pilots and ground crews. Later, I took pilots to the front lines so they could see how much better off they were than those poor devils who were fighting the Germans on the ground. I also took them to a collecting station where the wounded were treated. We eventually imbued these young kids with the idea that their prime task was support of the land campaign.

I took the position with General Bradley and all his subordinates that we knew how to use our weapon, the airplane, better than they did. I would not have tried to tell them how to use artillery; in return I did not want them telling me how to use tactical air power, and Bradley accepted that.

But how do you prove it? Only by doing. I wanted tactical air to perform in new ways that were better than the army ever visualized. We went into Normandy trying to find ways of supporting ground troops better than troops had ever been supported before.

On D-Day, the work of the tactical air force began in earnest. What happened earlier was important, but it was preliminary. If we failed now the army might fail. Waiting for the invasion, the Germans kept much of their armor back from the beaches. When troops and tanks moved up, we did our best to destroy them. The best example of our success is what happened to the famous Panzer Lehr division commanded by Lieutenant General Fritz Bayerlein. He had been Rommel's chief of staff in Africa and had commanded a tank division on the Russian front. Hitler personally chose him to lead this newest and strongest Panzer force. He got the best of everything in the way of men and equipment. We know a lot about Bayerlein because he kept a careful diary, which he still had when he was interrogated later as a prisoner.

The name "Panzer Lehr" fascinated me. Every time I heard it I was elated, and it became a happy target. That division was stationed 130 miles inland. Bayerlein was told that his job was to get to the invasion area, wherever it might be, and push the Allies back to the sea.

He got his orders to move up early on D-Day. He protested that he should wait until dark to avoid air attacks, but he was told to start immediately. As soon as he began to move, we attacked. He reported heavy casualties and the loss of many vehicles. His own car was shot up in the first of many attacks. Soon he was to have five drivers killed in quick succession in road attacks.

The second day he did not want to move again in the daytime but was given a firm order to proceed. He got moving at five a.m., and air attacks began half an hour later and continued all day. By evening he had lost a large part of his force before reaching the battle area. Instead of reaching the invasion area as planned, his force arrived forty-eight hours late, badly decimated and demoralized.

Our air attacks on German headquarters and command posts were very effective, according to Bayerlein when interrogated after capture. On D + 14, for example, Marauders, Thunderbolts and Typhoons swooped down on the headquarters of the Fifth Panzer Army and killed all the high-ranking officers except the commanding general.

Bayerlein was not the only commander to have trouble. In the area facing Bradley's First Army, every German division sent in to reinforce the front became disorganized and scattered. By listening to their radio talk we heard questions like "What do we do now?" and "Where do we go next?" It took one infantry division a whole week to travel less than one hundred miles by train, and then it had to make a long march on foot.

The Ninth and Tenth Panzer Divisions were in Poland. Beginning June 7, they began moving across Germany by train. They got to the French border and then were stalled. Most units took as long to travel the last 200 miles by road as they had to cover the first 1,300 miles by train. Other Panzer divisions took five days to cover 200 miles. In its war diary the German Seventh Army recorded on June 11: "Troop movements and all supply traffic to the army and within the army sector must be considered as completely cut off."

Such delays in reaching the battle area were the result of tactical air attacks on rail lines, trains, roads and bridges. Slowing down the German reinforcements was of the greatest importance to our side. In the planning before Normandy, British and American planners thought we could effect a landing. The big question was whether we could build up our forces before the Germans could send in strong reinforcements to defeat us in the beach area. The interdiction campaign of our joint air forces proved critical to this effort.

However, I do not want to make it sound as though our ground troops had an easy time. They never did. The Germans were experienced, and the hedgerow country in Normandy gave them a series of natural defenses. The ground fighting was very tough and at times brutal. Despite our air attacks the enemy moved up reinforcements at night and had sufficient strength to withstand strong efforts by both British and American armies to break out. The weather, as well as the terrain, was against us, and after its early success Allied progress was stalled.

General Eisenhower had insisted that the U. S. and British Strategic Air Forces be at his disposal. In this emergency the U. S. Eighth Air Force and RAF Bomber Command were diverted from their attacks on German industry to aid the Normandy breakout. The result was successful.

General Bayerlein again proved to be a good witness, because he and Panzer Lehr were directly under the heavy bomber attacks. His Panzer Lehr forces were temporarily stunned. As American troops began filtering through his lines, Bayerlein hid in a house for a while, then went on foot until he found a German mobile radio station. He reported to his next higher headquarters that nothing remained of Panzer Lehr. He had escaped with only the clothes he had on.

In the two weeks that followed, our tactical groups carried out the most important job they had during the war. As First Army fought its way to St. Lo our planes were always out in front, shooting or bombing every target that might have held up troops or tanks. The Germans sent in reinforcements in a desperate counterattack, which our fighters and fighter-bombers helped the Army to defeat.

General Eisenhower wanted to see the terrain at St. Lo for himself, and one day I flew him around the area, getting low enough so he could see how rough the country was. We had plenty of fighter cover overhead, and he enjoyed the experience with the enthusiasm of a young man.

In taking the extremely important town of St. Lo, Bradley had punched a wide hole in the enemy front. This paved the way for the breakthrough. Once the breakthrough was history, the great end run by the Third Army became possible.

A message from Major General Charles H. Corlett of III Corps said, "The presence of our aircraft over front-line troops has an immeasurable effect on their morale. When our airplanes are over the front line, the enemy use of artillery and mortars stops." This was typical of ground force recognition and appreciation of air power's contribution.

One of our next jobs was to attack airfields near Paris. The Germans had moved six or eight fighter groups to five fields there. They hoped to stop the Allied race across France. But our Tactical Air Force destroyed almost every plane that got into the air and knocked out the rest on the ground.

The success we had in supporting the ground troops was made possible by our communication system. Back in England I had realized that we would have to come up with something better in two-way communication between ground and air than had been the case in North Africa. The Microwave Early Warning (MEW) system provided the answer. It was devised in the Radiation Laboratory at M.I.T. and it was to make a notable contribution. Today radar is an accepted tool, but in those days it was new, and we were pioneering. Another radar device, known as SCR-584, permitted our controllers on the ground to know what was happening in the air out in front and direct pilots to where they were needed.

We also adapted the optical system of some Norden bombsights. Instead of a bombardier four or five miles up in the air using the sight to pinpoint a target on the ground, an air controller on the ground used it to pinpoint a pilot in the air and tell him his location in relation to his target on the ground.

This critical problem of identification can be specifically illustrated. A ground man talking to an airman might say, "There's an enemy tank over behind that tree." But from the air there might be a thousand trees. An airman on the ground talking pilot's language would say, "Do you see that church steeple?" because there would be only one church steeple and the pilot could see it. This could be solved only by having airmen as observers with the army units. Bradley understood this problem and agreed with my proposed solution.

The next step was to find pilots to put in the lead tanks. I called for volunteers. To my surprise, we had more volunteers than we needed. Pilots apparently wanted to get up to the front to see the land battles. The results proved invaluable in the St. Lo battle and became standard procedure.

In doing our best to be partners with the ground forces, we tried to supply them with all possible information about the enemy and what was going on behind their lines. What pilots saw was always a valuable and up-to-date source of information. Our photo-reconnaissance pilots took pictures every day the weather permitted, and they were duplicated and passed to ground commanders.

One of the best sources of information was "Ultra," which often gave us advance warning of German plans. This frequently gave us a more accurate knowledge of what was happening to the Germans than Hitler had. Time after time we would get copies of a message from Hitler to his field commanders, telling them to hold a certain position. But we already knew they had lost that position two days earlier. So Hitler did not always know where his front lines were. We also listened to radio conversations and heard the Germans talking about how they had been mauled by us. Hitler never got such information.

A German division commander would not tell his corps commander how he had been beaten up because he was afraid of being called a defeatist. The corps commander would not tell the Army commander for fear he would be thought subversive. And the Army commander was not going to tell his Army group commander, or the group commander would say "My God, what's this fellow trying to do, get me fired?"

Our pilots always had the problem of knowing just where our front-line troops were and where the enemy front line was. Lieutenant General "Lightning Joe" Collins was responsible for an idea that was of great help. His artillery would shoot colored smoke shells into the enemy lines, or where they wanted us to bomb. Our pilots could then bomb on the smoke.

Another good identification idea also came from the ground troops—putting colored panels on the top of tanks. Pilots could see the panels and knew those tanks were ours. The Germans caught on and began using the same color. So our tank forces changed colors each day. The panels were a lifesaver for our tanks in winter. Tanks covered with snow all look alike. During the Battle of the Bulge the panels were especially valuable.

As winter turned into the spring of 1945, more and more German troops surrendered. They often had only a choice between surrendering where they were or of trying to retreat by day and being slaughtered from the air.

In retrospect, I would say that of all the lessons we learned about tactical air operations, perhaps the most important is that the air commander, his group and squadron commanders must have sincere desire to become part of the ground team. The Army must, of course, have the same dedication to reciprocate.

This close liaison can come only from close day-by-day contact—especially at command levels; there must be almost instantaneous communication between ground and air and through all the chain of command.

Keeping flexible was also of the greatest importance. We had to be ready to invent new methods, try out new ways to attack, change what we had been doing to meet new conditions. The Luftwaffe lacked this flexibility, while we had it.

I have read with much interest the interrogations of German generals after they were captured. Invariably they said that Allied air power was one of the primary causes of their defeat. I am content to let it rest at that.

IMPACT

130 MPH HUMAN PICK-UP

See p. 48

CRISS-CROSSING THUNDERBOLTS GUARD 8th AF FORTS
See Strategic Campaign in Europe p. 2

IMPACT

CONTENTS
NOVEMBER, 1944

Confidential

ETO STRATEGIC SLUGGERS STILL SLUGGING HARD;

The tendency (noted in the June IMPACT) of our strategic air forces in Europe to concentrate an increasingly large proportion of their tonnages on tactical rather than on strategic targets, has lately begun to reverse itself. During the first half of October the Eighth Air Force dropped 12,857 strategic as against only 9,406 tactical tons. There are several reasons for this. First, the interdiction campaign in France (see pages 12-21) is over. Second, the greatly increased size of our tactical air forces, plus the fact that low-level attacks are more effective against personnel and small dispersed military targets than high-altitude bombardment, has relieved our heavies of much

of their tactical work. Third, new German industries have been earmarked for concentrated attacks. Fourth, the phoenix-like quality of German industry as a whole makes constant surveillance an absolute necessity. For example, with Ploesti gone and the Hungarian fields almost within the grasp of Russian armies, the Germans have redoubled their efforts to keep both their synthetic plants and their natural refineries operating. Two of the largest refineries in Hamburg are going at this writing, despite recent heavy attacks which had completely halted operations. Accordingly, tonnage statistics have shown oil to be the top priority for the Eighth for several months,

NEW TARGETS ARE ADDED TO THE OLD FAVORITES

followed in order by tank, truck, and ordnance works, then by aircraft and aero engine plants. Rail yards, a few months ago at the top, are now fourth on the target priority list.

Ordnance, tank, and truck works are now regarded vulnerable because of the enormous wastage by German armies on three fronts, which has more than consumed whatever excess productive capacity the enemy may have had prior to this; because of the numerous stresses to which an overburdened and overbombed industrial empire is now subject; and because of the loss of huge amounts of truck-producing capacity as a result of the liberation of France. Pictures of this phase of our strategic campaign will be found on pages 6 and 7.

The well-known recuperative ability of the German aircraft industry has been responsible for a continuance of the kind of attack pictured below. Production of conventional single-engine fighters has risen sharply during the summer and fall months, as has that of two types of jet-propelled aircraft, the Me-262 and Me-163. Linked with the campaign to reduce effectiveness of the latter are the blows at Peenemunde (see pages 4 and 5), one of five main producing centers for jet and rocket fuels, and long a station for experiments with robot bombs, rockets, glide bombs, and other types of controlled missiles.

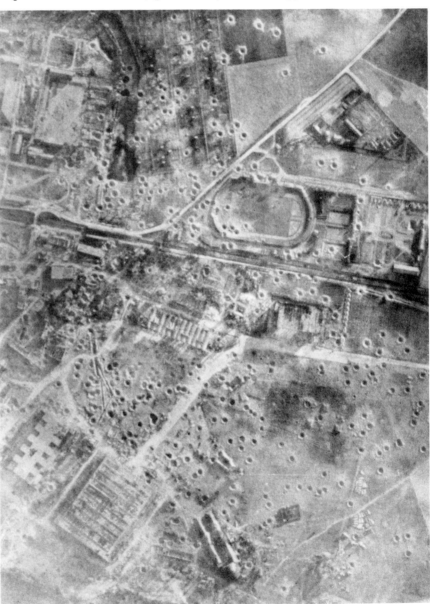

ROSTOCK. Oblique photograph at left shows the Heinkel Flugzeugwerke smoking from the 8th AF attack of 4 August, during which 148 bombers dropped 370 tons of GP and IB. Hit again with 311 tons on 25 August by 116 8th AF heavies, the northern half of the factory is shown (above) blanketed by these attacks. Large assembly shop (lower left) is severely damaged. Smaller shop next to it is slightly damaged. In center of picture two flight hangars, a large assembly shop, a paint shop and a canteen are all damaged. This plant has been making the He-111, now regarded obsolescent, and the He-219, a twin-engine long-range fighter.

Continued on next page

ELECTROSTATIC PLANT for manufacturing hydrogen peroxide was hit on 4 August by 221 B-17s dropping 522 tons (note craters from previous attacks). Center installation is the only one completed by the Germans. Characteristic circular embankment has been finished in unit at right, and preliminary work begun in unit at left. Both have since been abandoned.

ELECTROSTATIC PLANT (top of picture) is shown demolished in cover of 25 August during strike at electrolytic plant (bottom). Location of two main buildings is shown by dotted lines.

8th AF BLASTS PEENEMUNDE

One German target which is, in a sense, an industry in itself is Peenemunde, the huge experimental station on the shore of the Baltic. It is here that extensive tests in jet and rocket propulsion have been carried on for several years by the Germans, with projectiles being shot along the coast or out over the sea while they are tracked and tested for accuracy. Of particular interest at Peenemunde are the hydrogen peroxide plants shown here. Hydrogen peroxide (H_2O_2) in concentrated form, mixed with small quantities of alcohol, is an excellent propellant for pure rockets, which must draw on their own fuel for their supply of oxygen, as opposed to jet-driven projectiles, which depend on oxygen from the atmosphere. The mixture is forced into a combustion chamber under pressure, where it ignites in the presence of a catalyst such as potassium permanganate.

Two processes for manufacturing H_2O_2 are used at Peenemunde, the electrolytic and electrostatic. The former, and older, takes place in the rectangular buildings shown at the right, the latter (about which very little is known at present) in the round installations above and at the left. In the electrolytic process sulphuric acid is subjected to electrolysis, which turns it into persulphuric acid and hydrogen. Water is added to the persulphuric acid and this is distilled, giving off H_2O_2 with a top concentration of about 20 per cent. This is then subjected to further chemical treatment to bring it up to a strength of 85-90 per cent. Even at these high concentrations H_2O_2 is inherently stable. However, it is extremely delicate, and will disintegrate rapidly if exposed to heat, light, or dust.

In addition to Peenemunde, H_2O_2 plants at Friedrichshaven, Rheinfelden, Hollriegelskreuth, and Dusseldorf have been attacked in the campaign to reduce Germany's effectiveness in the use of rockets.

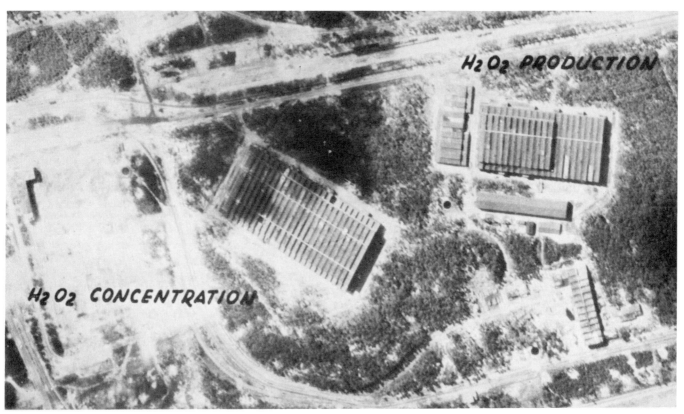

ELECTROLYTIC PLANT BEFORE. Photograph was taken on 4 August during strike attack on electrostatic plant shown at top of opposite page. This mission was only a small part of the day's operations of the 8th. A total of 1,417 heavies was dispatched, dropping 3,252 tons on three refineries, three aircraft factories, three airfields and port installations at Kiel.

ELECTROLYTIC PLANT AFTER. This photo shows installations still smoking from mission of 25 August. Two main electrolysis buildings have each sustained numerous direct hits. Three smaller buildings have been severely damaged. Attack was made by 146 B-17s which dropped 288 tons of GP, 77.5 tons of IB. The incendiaries were particularly effective.

Continued on next page

ORDNANCE PRODUCTION IN SILESIA AND RUHR BEING WHITTLED DOWN

WEIMAR ARMAMENT WORKS was attacked on 24 August by 129 8th AF heavies. Load was 175 1,000-lb. GP, 583 500-lb. GP and 279 500-lb. incendiaries, a total of 303 tons.

The bulk of German ordnance is centered in the two great iron and steel areas of the Ruhr and Silesia. The largest Ruhr plant is the Krupp works at Essen, followed by the Rheinmetall Borsig works at Dusseldorf. All the heavy instruments of war are made here, including large caliber guns and shells, aerial bombs, naval mine components, gun mounts, turrets and armor plate. Such heavy industrial areas have been pounded for several years, RAF pilots claiming that they can find their way down the Ruhr valley by following the pattern of flak bursts better than they can navigate in Piccadilly Circus on a foggy night.

Small arms manufacture is scattered among numerous firms throughout Germany, and small arms ammunition even more widely dispersed, no one firm producing more than a small percentage of total German output. One of the larger light armament plants is at Weimar/Buchenwald, shown under attack on this page. Rifles, self-propelled gun carriages, and armored military vehicles are made here. The target is made more attractive by the presence of a radio factory and a Gestapo headquarters and barracks, all of which were also hit.

WEIMAR AFTER. Reconnaissance photo shows tremendous damage. In the armament works (bottom center) seven of ten main workshops have been destroyed, the boiler house gutted, and other smaller buildings damaged. In the garage and storage area directly above 14 buildings were destroyed, nine severely damaged, and large numbers of trucks destroyed. The dotted rectangle to the right encloses a radio factory in which 13 buildings were destroyed and two gutted. This attack also destroyed seven buildings in the concentration camp next door. In the Gestapo headquarters, 11 buildings were destroyed.

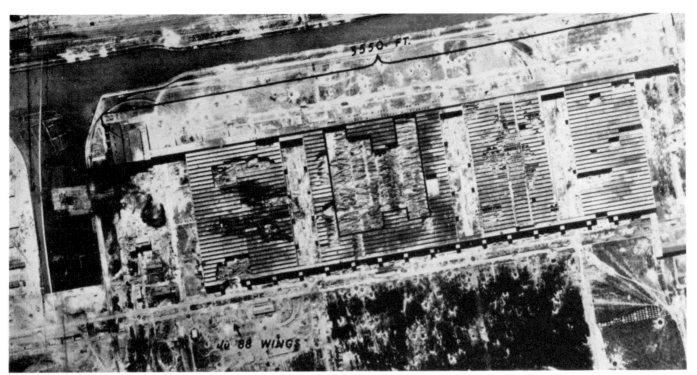

TRUCK, TANK FACTORIES SMASHED

The pictures on this page illustrate the growing severity of attacks against German tank and truck plants which have contributed strongly to the M/T shortage now plaguing the Wehrmacht. **Above** is shown the huge Fallersleben works as it looked after the 5 August mission when 85 Eighth AF heavies dropped 270 tons. It is estimated that six football games could be played simultaneously in the damaged area. Fallersleben produces flying bombs, Ju-88 parts, cars, jeeps, and has one of the largest metal pressing shops in Germany. **Below** is shown

the Borgward tank and truck plant in Bremen after 1,057 tons had been dropped on it by 394 8th AF heavies on 26 September. The main machine shop, assembly plant, foundry and finishing works all have suffered direct hits. This plant is one of six main truck producers in Germany. The other five have all been attacked as follows: Daimler Benz at Stuttgart (very heavily damaged on 5, 12 and 13 September), Ford at Cologne (a target for numerous attacks, this plant is so near the front lines that further production by it is not expected), Opel at Brandenberg (very severely damaged on 6 August), Bussing at Brunswick (damaged in several RAF saturation attacks), Auto Union at Chemnitz (severely damaged on 11 September).

OIL. Standard Oil Gennevilliers plant in Paris was hit on 22 June and 10 August by a total of 190 Eighth AF heavies dropping 743 tons. Tank cars shown above were caught beneath girders of grease manufacturing shop when roof fell in. Company had extensive storage facilities and a well-equipped mixing plant for raw materials. Both were virtually demolished.

OIL. Another view of Gennevilliers shows main works wrecked. Estimated monthly production of 2,200 tons and storage capacity of 13,000 tons were destroyed during these attacks, a serious blow to German armored force operations in France, as the chief products of this plant were lubricants and tank grease. Rail attacks made this loss almost impossible to replace.

AIRPLANE ENGINES. Hispano Suiza plant was taken over by Germans on entry into Paris, used for repair of 250 Mercedes and Daimler Benz engines a month. Hit by 8th AF bombs on 15 September and 31 December 1943, and plagued by constant sabotage by French workers, activity was thereafter limited to the finishing of engine parts from factories in the Pyrenees.

MOTOR VEHICLES. Renault plant in Paris produced 2,550 trucks, 500 tanks a month when taken over by Germans in June 1940. Blasted by the RAF and 8th AF, isolated by rail bombardment, chilled by strikes at fuel and electrical plants, denuded of its best workers, production skidded to zero in four years. The pictures below show details of 8th AF bomb damage.

TAKING WING, the XP-47N makes one of its experimental flights in preparation for its role as escort of very heavy bombers. Additional fuel tanks in inboard wing sections give new model far greater range than other types of fighter plane.

NEW, IMPROVED P-47 HAS MUCH MORE RANGE

The P-47N is an improved Thunderbolt whose new features extend the plane's combat radius of action so that it can be used to escort Very Heavy Bombers on long-range missions. This model has the same fuselage as the older types, and the P-47's characteristic stubby nose, but the wings have been altered in span and shape and the landing gear has been widened. New internal tanks add 100 gallons' fuel capacity in the inboard panels of each wing, which had to be lengthened about 18 inches; eight inches were then taken off each wing at the tip. The total wing spread was increased from 40 feet, nine inches to 42 feet, six inches. With 600 gallons in drop tanks, the P-47N will have a gas load of 1,170 gallons, and it is estimated that this will enlarge the Thunderbolt's combat radius to more than 1,200 miles. With CH-5 turbosupercharger, critical altitude is expected to be well above 30,000 feet.

The engineer's diagram on the lower half of the following page illustrates the principal features of the P-47N with the exception of the engine, which is an R-2800-C. The R-2800-B, now installed in the P-47D series, has a War Emergency Rating of 2,550 horsepower with water injection, using Grade 100/130 fuel. With water injection and Grade 100/150 fuel, the War Emergency Rating of this engine has been stepped up to 2,800 h.p. The R-2800-C power plant in the P-47N now has a WER of 2,800 h.p. when using a 50-50 mixture of water-alcohol injection and Grade 100/130 fuel. As IMPACT goes to press, tests are getting under way with Grade 100/150 and Grade 115/145 fuels. Based on War Emergency power obtainable with improved fuel with the R-2800-B engine, an increase in horsepower to above 2,800 can be logically expected with the R-2800-C power plant.

FLIGHT-LINE VIEW OF CURRENT P-47 (LEFT) AND XP-47N GIVES COMPARISON OF OLD WING WITH NEW

XP-47N SEEN from above, over Ohio grainland, shows pilot looking up at photo plane through teardrop canopy.

DIAGRAM of P-47N shows not only new major features but also smaller changes made in new model Thunderbolt.

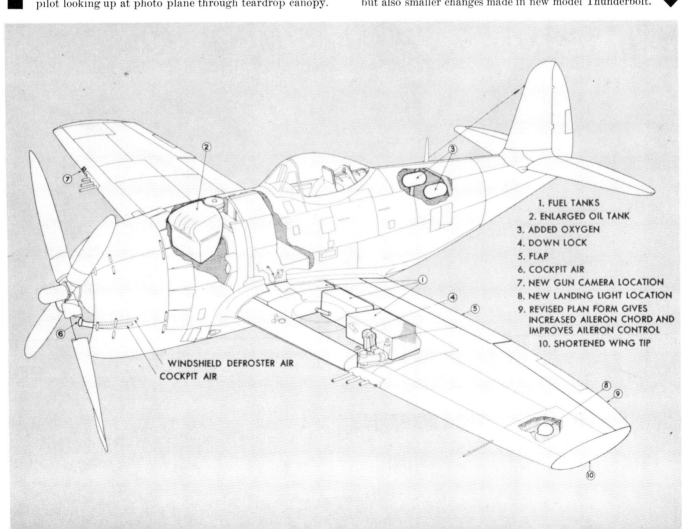

WINDSHIELD DEFROSTER AIR
COCKPIT AIR

1. FUEL TANKS
2. ENLARGED OIL TANK
3. ADDED OXYGEN
4. DOWN LOCK
5. FLAP
6. COCKPIT AIR
7. NEW GUN CAMERA LOCATION
8. NEW LANDING LIGHT LOCATION
9. REVISED PLAN FORM GIVES INCREASED AILERON CHORD AND IMPROVES AILERON CONTROL
10. SHORTENED WING TIP

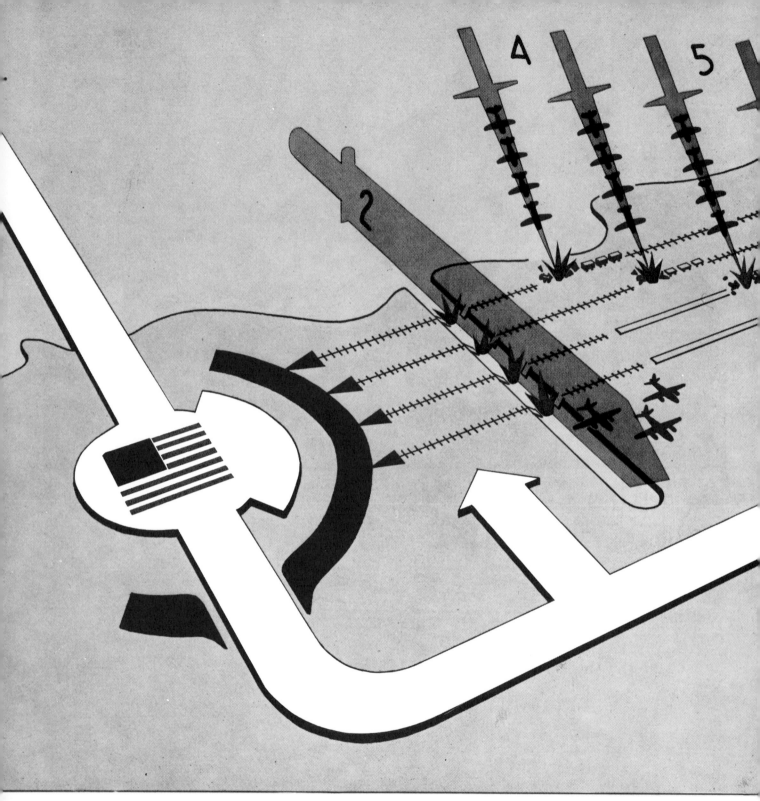

INTERDICTION

How Air Can Perform the Enormous Task of Isolating a Battlefield

Allied invasion plans were based on the theory that, once the Luftwaffe's back had been broken, a heavily defended coast could be breached by isolating the projected landing area through air attack directed against the enemy transportation facilities servicing that area. How this works, even when the troops and fortifications in the area are maintained by a rail network as formidable as that in northern France, is shown in the diagram above.

First step is to saturate rail yards, lowering operating efficiency and forcing the diversion of men and equipment to keep the system open for military traffic.

Second, a line of interdiction is set up by cutting all rail

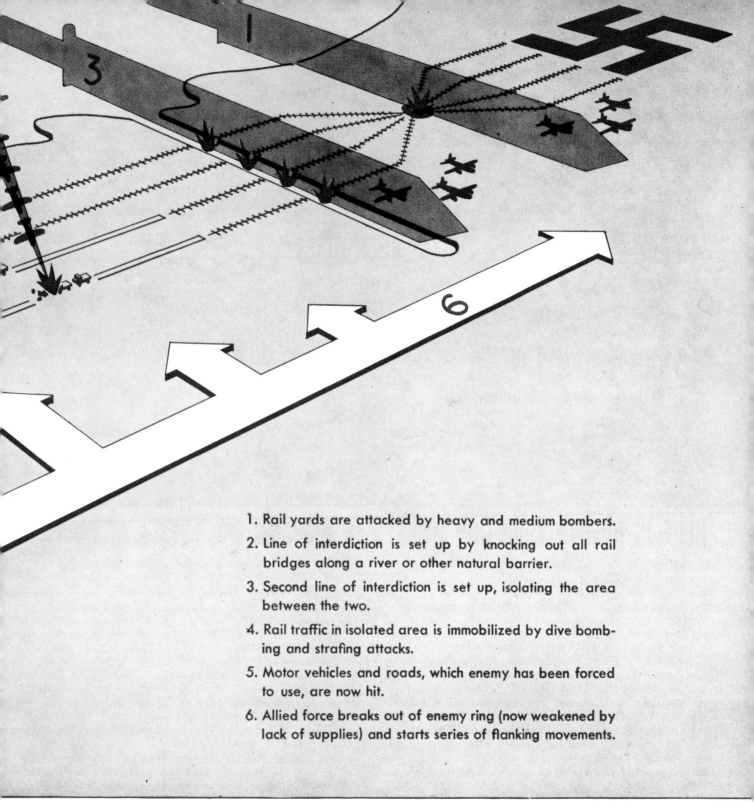

1. Rail yards are attacked by heavy and medium bombers.

2. Line of interdiction is set up by knocking out all rail bridges along a river or other natural barrier.

3. Second line of interdiction is set up, isolating the area between the two.

4. Rail traffic in isolated area is immobilized by dive bombing and strafing attacks.

5. Motor vehicles and roads, which enemy has been forced to use, are now hit.

6. Allied force breaks out of enemy ring (now weakened by lack of supplies) and starts series of flanking movements.

bridges across a natural barrier such as a river. This further hampers the flow of supplies by forcing the enemy to stop his trains at the river, unload into trucks or boats, and then load into different trains on the opposite side.

Third, another line of interdiction is established, forcing a double train-to-truck-to-train transfer, and creating a zone from which the locomotives and cars inside cannot escape, nor those outside get in.

Fourth, the irreplaceable rolling stock isolated in the zone of interdiction is clogged at certain points by bombardment, and then depleted by fighter attacks until the enemy is driven to road transport. This is undesirable from his point of view because trucks are less efficient than trains, because they are more vulnerable to strafing attack, but mostly because of the shortage of trucks, tires, and gas created by strategic bombing.

Fifth, the fighter attack shifts to the roads, forcing the enemy to operate only at night, in widely dispersed motor convoys, under rigid blackout conditions, all of which reduces the flow of supplies to the coast still further.

Sixth, a landing having been made, consolidated, and ground strength built up faster than the enemy's, all with the help of the transportation snarls described above, a series of end runs is undertaken to flank the enemy and annihilate him. To see how this actually worked in France, turn the page.

Continued on next page

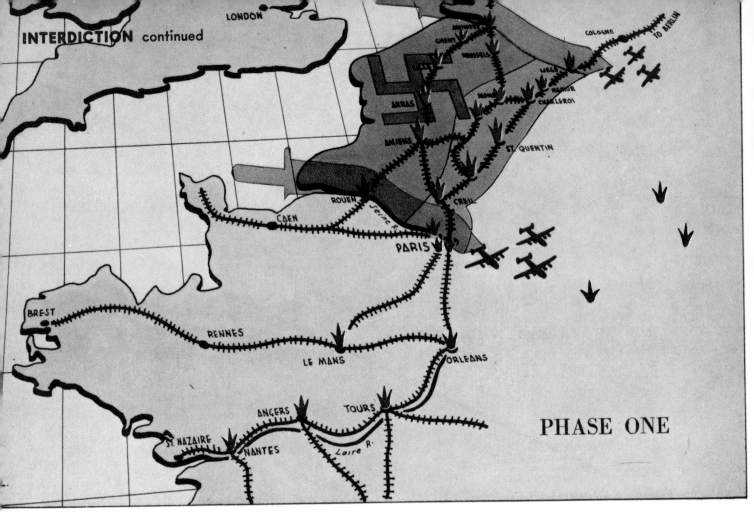

PHASE ONE

HERE IS HOW INTERDICTION WORKED IN WINNING THE BATTLE OF FRANCE

As in the theoretical example on the previous page, the invasion of France posed to Allied planners the problem of landing on a coast bristling with fortifications, and strongly garrisoned with troops which could rapidly be concentrated at any point through use of the densest rail system in the world.

Phase One (D minus 90 to D-Day). Air's first task was to prevent the movement of German troops from the Calais coast to Normandy as the invasion developed. The map above shows how the campaign began with bombardment of *all* the rail centers servicing these areas. This achieved the double purpose of improving our chances of securing a foothold without betraying where the attempt would be made. Next a line of interdiction was established between Paris and the sea by cutting bridges across the Seine river. Another such line was then set up along the Albert Canal and Meuse river. Purpose of this was to create a zone of interdiction between the two, and, by a further concentration of attacks within the zone, to heighten the impression that our landing would be made there. A glance at the map will show that the stage was now set. The bulk of the German forces was bottled between two lines of interdiction (shaded area around swastika) which at the same time cut off the real landing area from all directions except the south.

Phase Two (D-Day to D plus 55). Under heavy air cover landings were made, consolidated, and the Cherbourg peninsula captured in due course. However, a ring of enemy troops was thrown around our perimeter, successfully containing it for a period of weeks. The next job therefore was to build up sufficient force to break out, preventing at the same time a similar buildup by the enemy. Accordingly, another interdic-

tion line was established along the Loire river, linking up with the Seine line west of Paris and completely sealing off the battle area. A fourth line was set up east of Paris, extending (dotted red line) to the Loire line at Orleans. Meanwhile, a heavy war of attrition was being waged on the perimeter. We could afford it. Germany could not, as she had by now abandoned all attempts to move by rail, and her efforts at resupply and reinforcement by road (dark arrows) were subjected to devastating fighter and bomber attacks. Finally on 25 July a superior Allied force broke through the east end of the perimeter on the heels of a heavy aerial barrage.

Phase Three (D-plus-55 on). Once through the German ring, Allied armor poured into the vacuum behind it, forming a pocket at Falaise which was largely annihilated by air and ground attack. (Brittany, where a strong FFI movement aided by parachuting agents secured our flank, could largely be ignored.) No enemy stand was made at the Seine, the dangers of a second pocket being too apparent. Instead, the enemy retreated across it in good order despite a terrific jam-up and heavy losses on the banks of the river, whose bridges were still down (see picture on next page). Meanwhile the situation was further exploited by the brilliant and incredibly energetic flanking operations of our tank commanders, who were able to proceed day and night at top speed, aided by air cover and air supply (large red arrows), over roads less damaged than those being used by the enemy. A parallel advance by British and Canadian armies nearer the coast completed the undermining of the whole German defensive system in Northern France. Leaving garrisons at the principal ports, the Wehrmacht pulled out, shedding men and equipment at every step.

Confidential

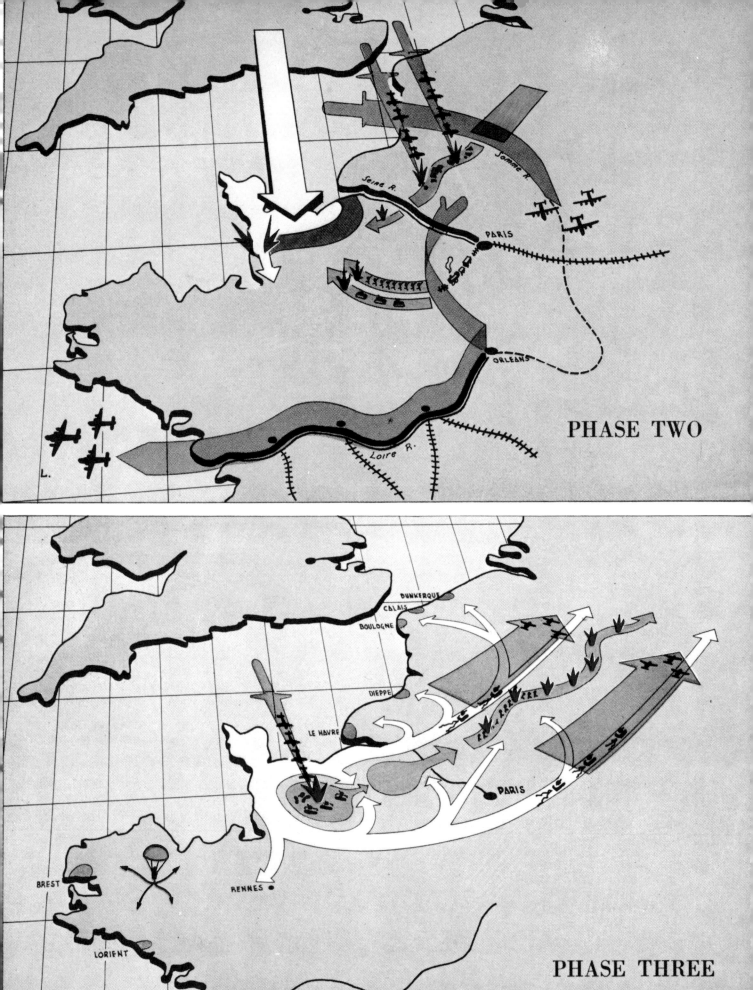

PHASE TWO

PHASE THREE

Continued on next page

SEINE RIVER INTERDICTION LINE

Just north of Paris at Conflans is situated the first of seven rail bridges which cross the Seine river, linking Brittany and Normandy with the great industrial areas of Eastern France, Belgium and the Ruhr valley. Attempts to establish a line of interdiction here were begun in May by the U. S. Ninth Air Force and the British Second Tactical Air Force. By 12 June each of these bridges was down, as shown by the pictures on the opposite page, also each of the thirteen road bridges which cross the Seine between Conflans and the sea. This formidable barrier not only enormously increased the difficulty of transporting German troops and equipment into the invasion area,

but it also made it almost impossible for those who escaped the Falaise pocket to get back without enduring withering attacks from the air while packed against the river bank and waiting to be taken across in boats.

Aircraft operating against the Seine bridges were almost entirely B-25s, B-26s, A-20s, P-47s and Typhoons, engaging in precision bombing, dive bombing and minimum-altitude attacks. Credit was shared about equally between bombers and fighters. An operational analysis found that dive bombing was about one-third as effective as minimum-altitude attack, but considerably less dangerous. For the latter to be successful, the bridge had to offer soft abutments, wooden scaffolding, or some other structure in which the bomb could stick while it exploded. Correct fusing is vital in all bridge attacks.

Continued on page 18

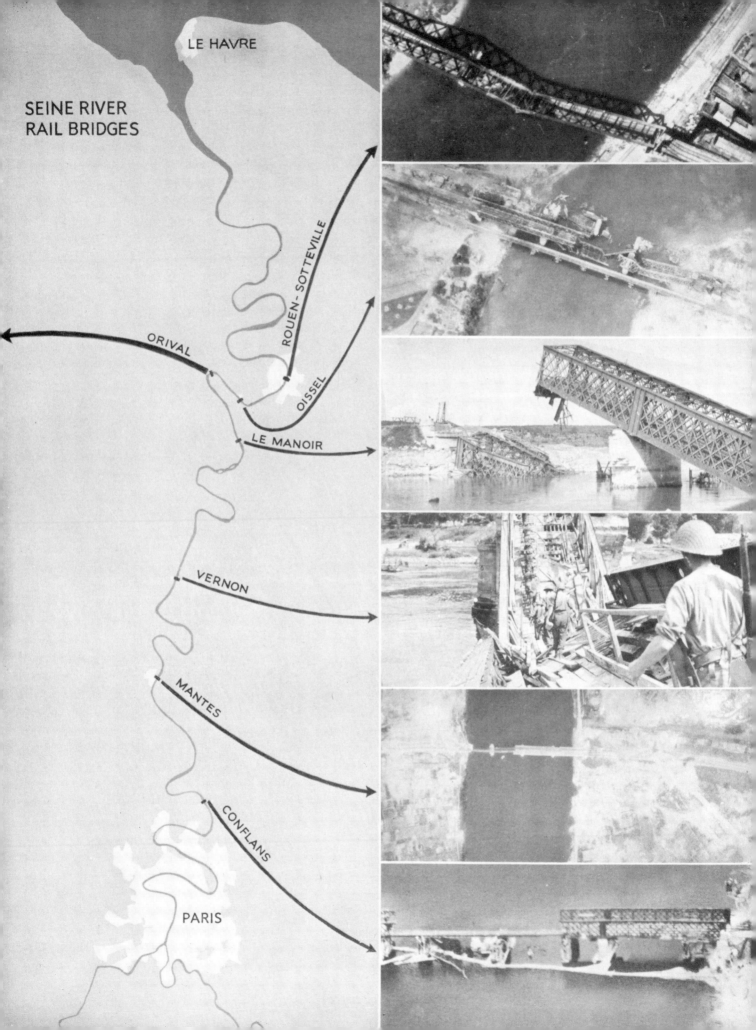

SEINE RIVER
RAIL BRIDGES

LE HAVRE

ORIVAL

ROUEN-SOTTEVILLE

OISSEL

LE MANOIR

VERNON

MANTES

CONFLANS

PARIS

No road safe for the Wehrmacht

GERMAN TANKS, M/T

Once the battle for the Normandy beaches was over and the galloping epidemic of Allied ground strength had begun to spread east and south, exploiting the enemy weaknesses created by the interdiction campaign, it became the mission of these armies to surround and destroy German military power in northern France before it could escape and reorganize itself. Occupation of further territory had become a secondary consideration. These pictures give a clue to what happened to the German 7th Army after it had been enclosed in the Falaise pocket. Hemmed in from the north by British and Canadians approaching Falaise, and from the south by Americans approaching Argentan, its only avenue of escape lay in the 13-mile gap between these towns. Interdiction, as shown on the preceding pages, had already paid enormous dividends in helping to set up this trap. The final task of air was to help kill the animal inside.

This was done by the closest kind of

WERE CUT TO PIECES

coordination between ground and air. Constant patrols provided reconnaissance for our ground commanders, allowing them to bring up superior force against any reported enemy concentrations. These were then dive bombed and strafed, and Allied armor, still in communication with the fighter planes, would move in for the kill. As the pocket became smaller and smaller, the congestion within became more acute, and Allied fighters worked the area over with increasing effectiveness. By 20 August, when all resistance collapsed, the entire pocket was carpeted with blasted guns, tanks and trucks.

The size of our air effort is shown by the 11,886 AEAF sorties flown on 18-20 August. German air activity during this period was microscopic. Allied vehicles could jam the roads by day with impunity, as the picture at the right (taken near Valognes on 24 August) graphically illustrates.

For us, bumper to bumper and perfectly safe

Continued on next page

BELFORT YARD BATTERED

One of the great natural barriers of Europe is the chain of the Vosges and Jura mountains which separates central France from southern Germany. Only passage through it is the Belfort Gap, where there is a confluence of rail lines and highways. Thus, the Belfort rail yard is an example of a perfect rail interdiction target. The Eighth Air Force hit it on 11 and 25 May, 17 July and 11 August. Two stages of the last attack, during which 76 heavies dropped 187 tons visually from 19,500 feet, are shown above and below. Cumulative results, right, show locomotive shops almost totally destroyed, transshipment shed and station shattered, all through lines cut.

LETHAL BLACK WIDOWS IN COMBAT GARB SEARCH SKIES OVER FRANCE FOR UNWARY JERRIES

1. ON NIGHT PATROL over France P-61 flies rectangular search pattern.

2. GROUND CONTROL reports "trade" at 9,000 ft., vectors P-61 in.

3. Ju-88 ZIG-ZAGS gently on course of 280° at 190 mph, altitude 9,000 ft. P-61

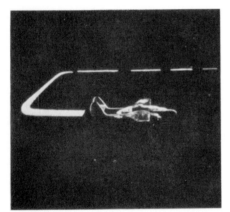

4. LONG BURST knocks fragments from Ju-88 which drops window and peels off sharply to port, diving to about 5,500 feet. P-61 loses its visual contact here.

5. CONTACT REGAINED at 7,500 feet on same vector of 280°, P-61 opens fire from

Confidential

THE WIDOWS BEGIN BITING

Two things have contributed to the development of the modern night fighter. One was the necessity, first for the British and later for the Germans, to defend against night bombardment missions which were saturating their cities. The other is radar, whose development to a point where it was really reliable in interception did not come until after the war had started. Accordingly, *existing* aircraft were radar equipped. In Britain the Beaufighter and later the Mosquito were so used, and proved big factors in making German night penetrations so expensive that they finally shrank to an insignificant dribble. When the ponderous RAF night missions began to roll, the Germans equipped interceptors—notably Me-110s and Ju-88s—with radar, causing an increase in RAF losses, which reached a climax over Nuremberg on the night of 30-31 March, 1944, when 66 RAF heavy bombers were shot down by German night fighters. For the past two years, the Battle of Radar has see-sawed with the Allies and the enemy developing new equipment and countermeasures.

Because our need has not been so urgent, the AAF has not concentrated on the development of night fighter organizations on a scale comparable to those of the British and Germans. Now, however, we have in operation in both Europe and the Pacific the first airplane specifically designed for night fighting—the P-61 "Black Widow." In addition, we have developed an efficient new radar ground control setup, the MEW (Microwave Early Warning). It has been the major radar reporting and control equipment since it first went to work covering the Normandy D-Day.

With an efficient height finder, MEW can pick up hostiles at considerable ranges and vector a P-61 (or any night fighter) to them. Under good conditions, this can bring in a P-61 close enough for it to establish a visual. More commonly it would simply get the fighter to a point where its own airborne radar (SCR-720) could take over. As soon as the kill is made, ground control can take over again, either vectoring the fighter back to base or putting it onto a new hostile.

(Functioning of SCR-720 was described in IMPACT, Volume 2, Number 5. For detailed operational information on MEW, see RADAR Magazine, Number 3 and Number 5.)

The P-61, an aircraft considered far superior to the night fighter version of the A-20 which it supplants, faces a particularly busy future in the war in the Pacific. As we move nearer Japan we must be prepared for the possibility that the enemy may muster more effective air assaults than he has been capable of recently. Part of our preparation is the P-61. How this aircraft goes about an interception is illustrated in the model sequence below showing a Ju-88 killed by a P-61 over Normandy on 6 August. Distances between planes have been shortened because of space limitations.

makes a visual contact from 1,000 feet away and closes rapidly to a range of 400 feet.

500 ft. 5° below and dead astern. Short burst scores several direct hits on the Ju-88.

6. ENEMY MUSHES completely out of control to port and explodes in a burst of flame. Burning parts fell into the overcast below; nobody was seen to bail out.

P-47 STRAFES A WINDING MOUNTAIN HIGHWAY IN SOUTHERN FRANCE

P-38's NOSE-BORNE CAMERA RECORDS

THUNDERBOMBERS

P-38 "Droopsnoot" Photo Plane Follows MAAF
P-47s To Obtain Striking Low-Level Obliques

The three pictures shown here were taken from a special "droopsnoot" P-38, rigged up by the MAAF to obtain the rarest thing in aerial combat photography—good, clear shots of dive bombing and strafing. The pictures show attacks by the MAAF's favorite aircraft for rough work at low level, the P-47, dubbed the "Thunderbomber" in the theater. Thunderbombers have seen very heavy action recently in Northern Italy and Southern France. In June, Thunderbombers of the Mediterranean

STRAFING OF RAIL YARDS IN ITALY

CAUSEWAY AT VIRGIL'S HOME TOWN, MANTUA, IS "THUNDERBOMBED"

Allied Tactical Air Force flew 5,001 effective sorties, dropping 2,931 tons of bombs; in July, 4,593 effective sorties, 1,929 tons; in August, 7,737 effective sorties, 2,516 tons. During these operations, the Tactical Air Force lost 120 planes and 118 were damaged. There were 23 enemy planes destroyed plus three probables. M/T columns, trains, marshalling yards and, during the Southern France invasion, gun positions and radar stations, have been priority targets.

The MAAF modification which has made a P-38 into a whirlwind photo plane that follows P-47s in their dives, is a plate glass nose resembling that of a B-17. Extending back as far as the camera and the battery plumbing station, this nose is equipped with a photographer's seat and the usual instruments for a bombardier. The camera is an AK 22 with a twelve-inch lens. The "droopsnoot" stays about 1,000 yards behind the combat planes and comes to the IP at an altitude of about 13,000 feet. The photo plane dives just as the last bomb-carrying fighter releases its load: The P-38 goes in lower than the P-47s, usually to 600 feet (with I.A.S. at about 550). This is dangerous above a target strongly defended by flak. One such P-38 was hit near Turin. It crash-landed behind the Allied lines. Pilot and cameraman were unhurt.

BURNING PLOESTI

These captured German films recorded what went on (in daylight) under those great, mushrooming smoke columns so often shown in aerial photos taken during AAF attacks on Ploesti's refineries. The films do not identify individual refineries.

Confidential

P-47s TAKE FIRST CARRIER RIDE INTO COMBAT

P-47s WITH PILOTS AND CREW CHIEFS STAND INSPECTION AT OAHU, HAWAII, BEFORE LONG TRIP TO SAIPAN

From Hawaii to Saipan They Went to Hit Japs

One more example of AAF-Navy cooperation is the case of the 71 P-47s ferried to Saipan last June for 7th Air Force operations against the Japs on Saipan, Tinian and Rota. The secret nature of the operation has made it impossible to tell the story until now. It was the first time P-47s were thus used in the Pacific and also the first time, so far as is known, that P-47s were catapulted from carriers.

Preparations for this historic trip were completed in Hawaii at Bellows Field, Oahu, where the land birds were given a final preening for their ocean migration. With machine guns installed, and motors checked, on 16 May they were lined up for inspection by the Commanding General. At the same time, maintenance equipment and supplies were sent by truck to Pearl Harbor for subsequent shipping to Saipan. The planes themselves were flown the short distance to Ford Island naval base, and hoisted aboard two escort-type aircraft carriers.

With planes lashed firmly to their decks, the carriers embarked on 5 June, stopping at Eniwetok for refueling. Despite a Jap attack, the voyage was made without mishap, except that a motion picture screen accidentally fell and injured the prop of a P-47. A Navy TBF from a friendly base flew in a replacement. Mechanics made frequent checks on the planes to keep them in shape for the coming takeoff.

On 23 June, near the coast of Saipan, all planes were successfully launched. It took less than two minutes to launch each plane.

BEING HOISTED ABOARD deck of escort-type carrier at Ford Island, Pearl Harbor, this is one of the 71 P-47s that took the trip.

Continued on next page

DURING ATTACK BY FOUR JAP PLANES, BOMBS SPLASH PERILOUSLY NEAR CARRIER WITH LOAD OF P-47s

DESTINATION REACHED, THIS P-47 ON CATAPULT DECK IS READY FOR LAUNCHING FROM THE CARRIER

CARRIER CREWMEN CROUCH TENSELY AS P-47 GETS AWAY SUCCESSFULLY OVER A GLITTERING OCEAN

CARRIER IS BUZZED IN FAREWELL SALUTE AS THE P-47s HEAD FOR THEIR NEW LAND BASE ON SAIPAN

MEN OF THE 21st WATCH HOMECOMING PLANE

HAULING WATER, this coolie replenishes tanks that supply a 21st Photo Squadron laboratory at an advanced base in China.

FAR-FLYING 21st

In the field of aerial sleuthing the 21st Photographic Squadron does a job that in earthbound detective circles would tax the talents of Sherlock Holmes and Perry Mason combined. For its beat, the 21st has nearly four million square miles of Far Eastern territory, shown below. Most of it is Jap-held. Upon clues furnished by the 21st, a good part of our battle strategy against Japan is based.

This outfit was activated on 19 December 1942 at Peterson Field, Colorado Springs. Each department — Laboratory, Camera Repair and Engineering — went through its paces as near to field conditions as possible. By 1 July, 1943, the 21st, joined by its planes and pilots, had reached India. For jumping the Hump, supplies were divided into three parts, in case one cargo plane failed to get through. But no supplies were lost.

In China, the Squadron was divided into three flights, and later into four. "A" Flight absorbed the 9th Photo Squadron which had been stationed there for some seven months, and at Kunming set up headquarters for the entire outfit. "B" Flight was set up at Kweilin, and covered the Canton-Hongkong, and Hankow-Wuchang area, with occasional runs to Shanghai. In October 1943, when it became necessary to get regular cover on Formosa, a smaller forward base was established at Suichwan, known as Flight "C." From there, also, the Squadron's first extremely long mission was flown, covering Sasebo and Nagasaki in the Jap homeland—a hazardous roundtrip of about 2,200 miles.

Next spring "C" made its historic mission to Corregidor (page 37)—the first time it had been covered since the dark days of 1942. The flight lasted nine hours. On 17 April a fourth flight, "D," was located at Liangshan to cover Northeast China, as well as Mukden (pages 34, 35). "D's" runs are long and rugged, often staged from primitive forward fields where planes are laboriously refueled from five-gallon cans.

AREA COVERED by 21st is shown below, along with original locations of its four Flights, indicated by AAF plane insignia.

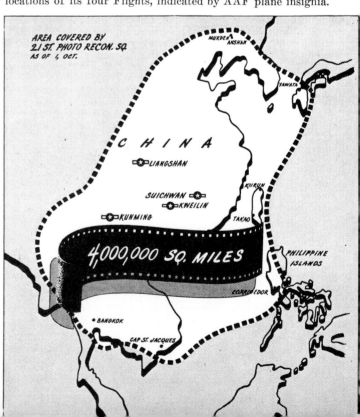

AREA COVERED BY 21ST PHOTO RECON. SQ. AS OF 4 OCT.

MUKDEN/ANSHAN
YAWATA
C H I N A
LIANGSHAN
KIIRUN
SUICHWAN
KWEILIN
TAKAO
KUNMING

4,000,000 SQ. MILES

PHILIPPINE ISLANDS
CORREGIDOR
BANGKOK
CAP ST. JACQUES

SQUADRON MAKES RECON HISTORY

WATER-HAULING FROM A RIVER IS ANOTHER STEP IN KEEPING 21st LABS RUNNING OVERTIME IN CHINA

EXCELLENT PROTECTION, even for jeeps, against enemy planes is afforded by limestone caves at one base.

PHOTO LAB at forward base, handy to water supply, is located against one of the jagged limestone hills typical of the area.

Confidential

Continued on next page

GASOLINE TRUCK waits to refuel a plane of the 21st, as camera repairmen complete work. In background are ruins of headquarters from which Japs were driven by Flying Tigers.

FLIGHT LINES for both charting and reconnaissance photography are carefully drawn during briefing to permit the pilot to obtain maximum coverage with minimum time over the target.

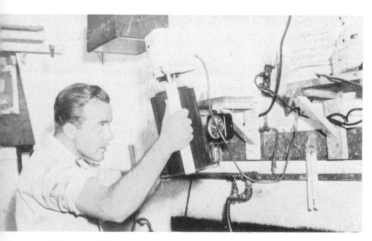

INSTALLING MAGAZINES of film on F-5, "Frantic," camera repairmen get plane ready. The "Frantic" flew long range mission to Yawata, has flown more than 100 combat missions.

READY FOR TAKE-OFF, is Major G. H. Fulcher, former operations officer, and now Commanding Officer of Squadron. This particular mission was flown over Canton and Hongkong.

AFTER MISSION, developer checks negatives during washing process. Below: Squadron S-2, Major W. Nicholls, interrogates Lt. Col. John C. Foster on his return from Saigon mission.

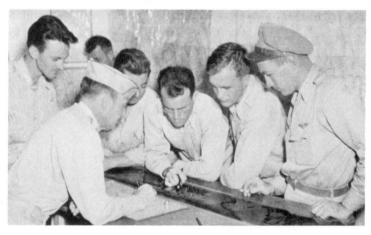

FOR RUSH PRINTING, pilot and S-2 Officer watch as P.I.'s pick negatives. Below: Personnel of photogrammetry section complete essential charts from trimetrogon photographs.

FRUITS OF THEIR LABORS — MUKDEN TO MANILA

Like a big game hunter bringing home a hide is the photo reconnaissance pilot bringing home his film. It is the trophy of his kill. More than that, it leads to bigger kills. It may save his comrades' lives, and is vital to the progress of war. Here, and on the next four pages, are some of the prize pictures taken by the 21st Squadron whose hunting ground includes Burma, Thailand, French Indo-China, Philippines, Hainan, Formosa, Japan, Korea, Northern and Eastern China.

The outfit which produces this coverage certainly justifies the term "far-flung." From Flight "A" to Flight "B" is 500 air miles, to Flight "C" 800 miles, to Flight "D" 900 miles. Each Flight operates independently under a Flight C.O., but is closely coordinated with Flight "A" which is Squadron Headquarters. Each Flight flies tactical missions as requested by the Wing to which it is attached for operations, and at the same time, flies strategic missions requested by the 14th AF. All laboratories take great pride in their work, the "A" lab working 24 hours a day on three shifts. From 12 July 1943 to 12 July 1944, the Squadron for all flights ran 549 missions of which only 4.5% were duds due to engine or mechanical failure, and 17% due to bad weather. Making the above record, only one pilot was lost, on a non-combat mission.

TAKAO This Formosa harbor is a major staging point for Jap convoys, and was a target of big U. S. Naval attacks in mid October. Ships here are (1) suction dredger, (2) tanker 400'/500', (3) M/Vs 200'/500', (4) M/Vs 200'/400'.

Continued on next page

NORTH MUKDEN Buildings here had been reported as a fuselage and assembly plant. But on 19 June this valuable photo revealed that plant is for modifications and repairs. Key: (1, 11) administration, (2, 3, 6, 7) hangars—some under construction, (4) workers' quarters, (5) power, (8, 9) workshops, (10) probable foundry, (12) boiler house. Lower left: ancient Manchu tomb. Round trip for this mission was 2,150 miles, all but 90 of them over enemy territory.

EAST MUKDEN Also taken on 14 June, this area is near North Mukden airfield. Key: (1) AA battery, (2) Manchuria Airplane Mfg. Co.—A/C assembly, (3) Mukden arsenal, (3a and 3c) explosive storage and probable shell loading, (3b) probable components loading plant, (4) Manchuria Iron Works, (5) machine tool plant, (6) ceramics plant. Aircraft count here exceeded any photographed at any single field by the 21st Squadron in Asia. They numbered 126.

Continued on next page

OKAYAMA Taken on 25 August, this covers a major Formosa target hit later by 20th Bomber Command B-29s. On first mission on 14 October, 106 B-29s hit Okayama A/C plant with 785.46 tons. All air strips in area were inoperable due to bomb damage, at least 50 aircraft on ground were destroyed or damaged. On second mission two days later Heito and other Formosa targets were hit by 69 B-29s. Of these, 32 hit Okayama, had no losses. Of 34 major buildings at target, all but two have now been destroyed.

TARGET AREA NO 1
AIRCRAFT PLANT

SOUTH HANGAR &
BARRACKS AREA

EAST HANGAR
& ADMIN. AREA

UNDERGROUND
STORAGE

TARGET AREA NO.2
OKAYAMA AIRDROME

1000   0   1000   2000

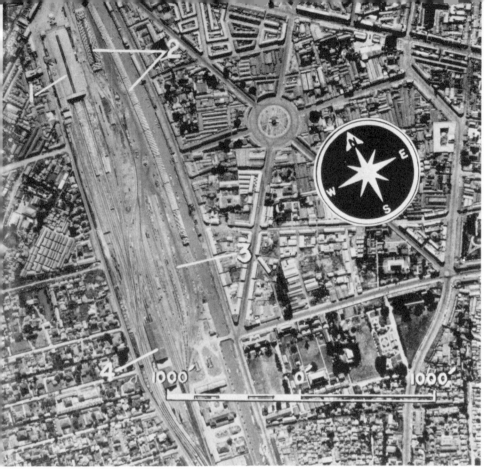

BANGKOK Above, excellent coverage of railyards in Thailand's capital shows (1) terminus station, (2) freight sheds, very poorly camouflaged in comparison to German methods, (3) railroad sidings, (4) locomotive sheds.

CORREGIDOR Below, first coverage of Philippines since 1942 shows on 12 May 1944 (1) Corregidor, (2) Caballo island, (3) Caballo bay, (4) Kindley Field, (5) Seaplane base, (6) north channel, (7) Bataan.

CAP ST. JACQUES Above, near Saigon in French Indo-China, this harbor was hit by 14th AF Liberators, four days before this picture was taken on 3 March. Big tanker is still burning from the attack.

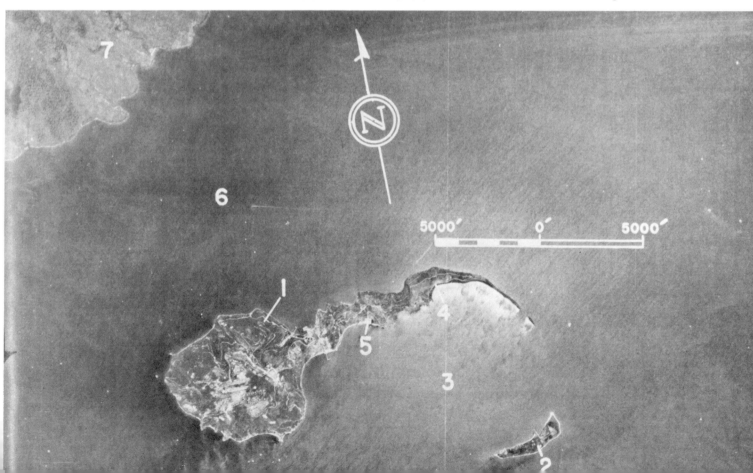

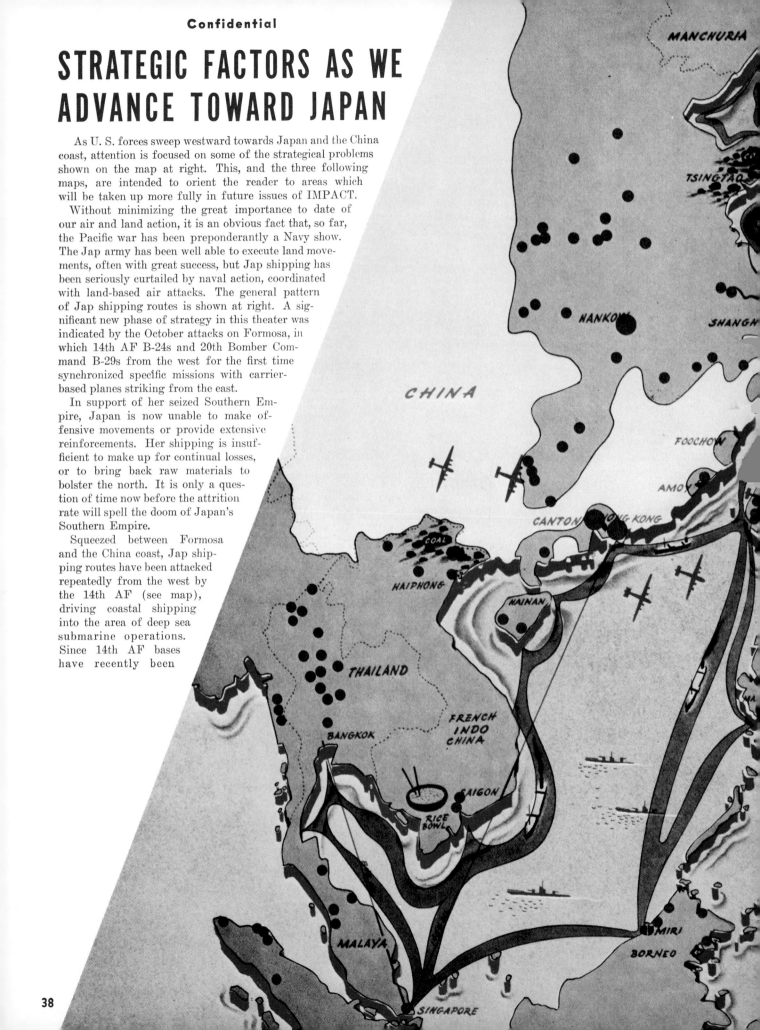

STRATEGIC FACTORS AS WE ADVANCE TOWARD JAPAN

As U. S. forces sweep westward towards Japan and the China coast, attention is focused on some of the strategical problems shown on the map at right. This, and the three following maps, are intended to orient the reader to areas which will be taken up more fully in future issues of IMPACT.

Without minimizing the great importance to date of our air and land action, it is an obvious fact that, so far, the Pacific war has been preponderantly a Navy show. The Jap army has been well able to execute land movements, often with great success, but Jap shipping has been seriously curtailed by naval action, coordinated with land-based air attacks. The general pattern of Jap shipping routes is shown at right. A significant new phase of strategy in this theater was indicated by the October attacks on Formosa, in which 14th AF B-24s and 20th Bomber Command B-29s from the west for the first time synchronized specific missions with carrier-based planes striking from the east.

In support of her seized Southern Empire, Japan is now unable to make offensive movements or provide extensive reinforcements. Her shipping is insufficient to make up for continual losses, or to bring back raw materials to bolster the north. It is only a question of time now before the attrition rate will spell the doom of Japan's Southern Empire.

Squeezed between Formosa and the China coast, Jap shipping routes have been attacked repeatedly from the west by the 14th AF (see map), driving coastal shipping into the area of deep sea submarine operations. Since 14th AF bases have recently been

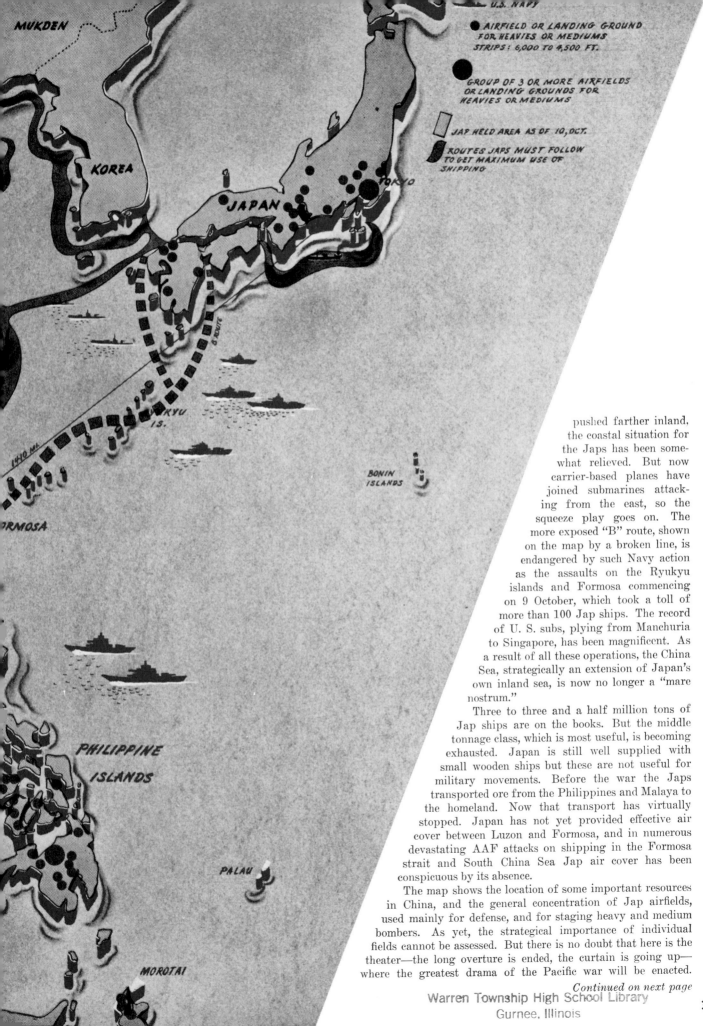

MUKDEN

KOREA

JAPAN

TOKYO

A ROUTE

B ROUTE

RYUKYU IS.

1410 MI.

FORMOSA

BONIN ISLANDS

PHILIPPINE ISLANDS

PALAU

MOROTAI

pushed farther inland, the coastal situation for the Japs has been somewhat relieved. But now carrier-based planes have joined submarines attacking from the east, so the squeeze play goes on. The more exposed "B" route, shown on the map by a broken line, is endangered by such Navy action as the assaults on the Ryukyu islands and Formosa commencing on 9 October, which took a toll of more than 100 Jap ships. The record of U. S. subs, plying from Manchuria to Singapore, has been magnificent. As a result of all these operations, the China Sea, strategically an extension of Japan's own inland sea, is now no longer a "mare nostrum."

Three to three and a half million tons of Jap ships are on the books. But the middle tonnage class, which is most useful, is becoming exhausted. Japan is still well supplied with small wooden ships but these are not useful for military movements. Before the war the Japs transported ore from the Philippines and Malaya to the homeland. Now that transport has virtually stopped. Japan has not yet provided effective air cover between Luzon and Formosa, and in numerous devastating AAF attacks on shipping in the Formosa strait and South China Sea Jap air cover has been conspicuous by its absence.

The map shows the location of some important resources in China, and the general concentration of Jap airfields, used mainly for defense, and for staging heavy and medium bombers. As yet, the strategical importance of individual fields cannot be assessed. But there is no doubt that here is the theater—the long overture is ended, the curtain is going up—where the greatest drama of the Pacific war will be enacted.

Continued on next page

AS SHIP LOSSES MOUNT, JAPS RELY ON CHINA'S RAIL SYSTEM

With ship losses soaring, the Japs are forced to depend more on the rail system shown above to transport troops and supplies to armies in China, and to send home raw materials. Major rail arteries are shown by heavier tracks. These connect Manchuria, home of the Kwantung Army and its arsenals, with the vital Yangtze river route and with the iron and coal of North China. Another major line goes through Manchuria, down to the Korean port of Fusan, enabling Japs to use the relatively safe, short route across the Korean Strait to the homeland. Bomb bursts on map show how 14th AF has been ripping up rails in Southeastern China and blasting river traffic. As a result, many Jap troops have had to go by truck or by foot to fighting zones. Thus, the battle of supply lines in China, as in Europe, becomes a crucial part of our war strategy.

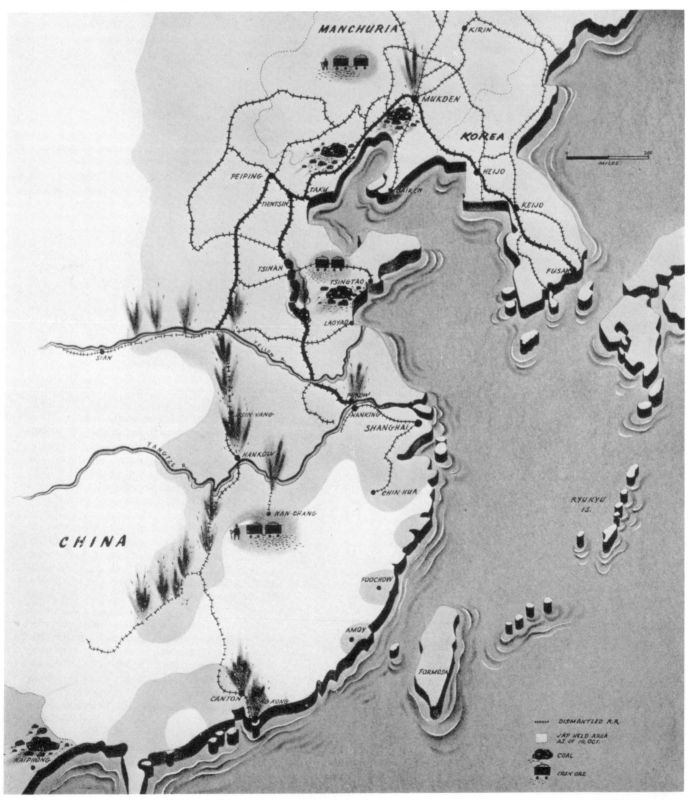

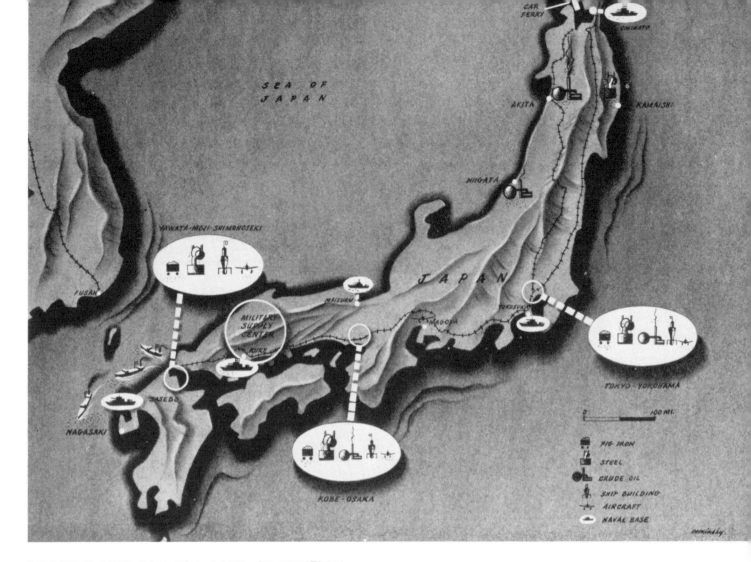

INDUSTRY MAY ROT FOR LACK OF MATERIAL

Above are indicated some principal Japanese industries, and three main areas where they are located. These may soon be rendered impotent, both by AAF bombs and because Jap shipping losses are depriving them of raw materials. Also, contributing to Japan's transportation nightmare is the fact that she depends heavily upon one major, over-burdened rail route, shown above. This tenuous backbone of land transport links coal and steel areas of the north and south with the big industrial and population centers of central Japan. It also serves ports of entry from the mainland, and via car ferry, connects with the northern island of Hokkaido, rich in coal and lumber. Coastal vessels carried the bulk of this traffic until Japan diverted ships to supply her crumbling empire.

FORMOSA: JAP BASTION AND SUPPLY BASE

Formosa is prized by the Japs as a supply base, as an aircraft staging and training center, as a bastion guarding Jap shipping lanes, as an air base for defense of China and the Philippines, and for its own natural resources. It produces, roughly, one-third of Japan's sugar, nine per cent of her copper, 15 per cent of her aluminum. Its harbors at Kiirun and Takao are useful to convoys for assembling and fueling.

For all these reasons, Formosa was pasted by B-29s and carrier-based planes in adroitly coordinated attacks in mid October. Main targets, and type of attack, are shown at right. Greatest damage was done at Okayama (page 36). But the No. 1 reason for blasting Formosa was to help isolate the Philippines in preparation for the historic event of 20 October.

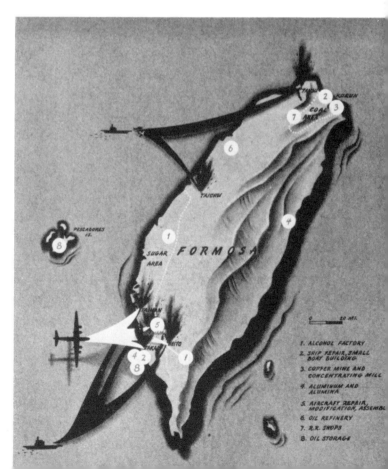

1. ALCOHOL FACTORY
2. SHIP REPAIR, SMALL BOAT BUILDING
3. COPPER MINE AND CONCENTRATING MILL
4. ALUMINUM AND ALUMINA
5. AIRCRAFT REPAIR, MODIFICATION, ASSEMBLY
6. OIL REFINERY
7. R.R. SHOPS
8. OIL STORAGE

MAP SHOWS WHERE PHILIPPINES TOOK PRE-INVASION POUNDING

GRAND STRATEGY UNFOLDS—WE ARE IN PHILIPPINES

The significance of strategic factors discussed on preceding pages was illuminated on 20 October when the latest step in our Far East strategy placed us back in the Philippines. Here was the pay-off for a series of seemingly unrelated operations: the neutralizing of Formosa by coordinated carrier-based and 20th Bomber Command attacks; the relentless war on Jap shipping by the 14th AF, FEAF, and the Navy; the attacks on Jap industry from Manchuria to Yawata. All of this, to be sure, was directed towards the final conquest of Japan. But at the same time these operations contributed definitely to the Philippine invasion.

For at least six weeks before the landing at Leyte, combined AAF and Naval action was concentrated specifically on pounding the Philippines. At left are shown the general areas where most of these attacks occurred. Planes and carriers are used on the map only to symbolize the type of attack (land- or carrier-based). All carrier-based attacks are by the Third Fleet, unless otherwise designated, and no action after 21 October is indicated. Numbers are keyed thus:

1. 1-6 Sept. Philippines on 1 September were bombed for first time since 1942 by 57 5th AF heavies of the FEAF, hitting targets in Davao area (IMPACT, Vol. 2, No. 10). Attacks were continued daily until 6 Sept., and thereafter intermittently. Attacks on Buayan airfield by B-25s began on 6 September.

2. Through September Jap shipping was continuously bombed near these targets by PBYs and FEAF B-24s.

LANDING BEACH AT LEYTE, NORTH OF DULAG, SHOWS TYPICAL JAP INSTALLATIONS. KEY: ABOVE, RIGHT.

LANDING AREA at Leyte was photoed 14 to 16 September. By 25 October U. S. forces had won 25 miles of coast, and three airfields, at Tacolban, Dulag, and San Pablo.

3, 4. 12-14 Sept. At Catabato, Leyte and in the Visayas 486 Jap planes were destroyed —164 in the air, 322 on ground. Navy reported, "Enemy's non-aggressive attitude at Mindanao is incredible."

5. 20-21 Sept. Heavy attacks on Clark and Nichols fields, Manila harbor, and Cavite naval base, destroyed warehouses, railroad equipment, oil storage, harbor installations. More than 50 classified ships and one sub were sunk. 169 planes were shot down, 180 were damaged on ground.

6. 11 Oct. At Appari 10 to 15 aircraft were destroyed on ground. On 18 October 15 destroyed on ground at Laog.

7. 15-18 Oct. Our planes were aggressively intercepted by Zekes, Oscars and Tonys of which 80 to 90 were destroyed in air, 60 to 70 on ground. An extra 30 planes were shot down in the vicinity.

8. 20 Oct. FEAF, RAAF, units from 3rd and 7th Fleet, and Australian Naval Squadrons covered the Leyte assault.

9. 17-21 Oct. Striking first in the Luzon area, and then coming down to cover landing operations at Leyte, our planes shot down 77 enemy aircraft in air, and 117 on ground. 7th Fleet units at Leyte, Cebu and Panay also shot down six enemy aircraft on 20 October.

--- **KEY TO ANNOTATIONS BELOW** ---

⚐ AUTOMATIC AA POST (EMPTY)	⚐ MACHINE GUN	⚑ OBSERVATION POST
⚒ ARTILLERY EMPLACEMENT	⚐ RIFLE PIT OR FOXHOLE	⚑ AMMUNITION STORAGE
⚒ COVERED ART. EMPLACEMENT	⊡ COMMAND POST	⚏ TRENCH
⚓ PILLBOX	⚐ SEARCHLIGHT	⚏ ANTI-TANK TRENCH

AREA OF U. S. LANDINGS

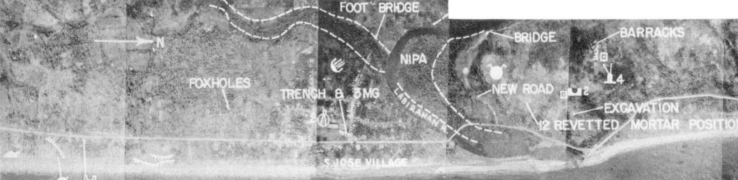

EACH OF BOTH LANDING AREAS COVERED ABOUT THREE MILES OF COAST. DATE OF PHOTO, 14-16 SEPTEMBER

JAP PLANES BURN ON IWO JIMA AIRFIELD DURING 7th AF ATTACK

IWO JIMA

While other air forces and the Navy make history elsewhere in the Far East, the 7th AF has concentrated on neutralizing the Bonins. One of its main targets is Iwo Jima, only 670 miles from Tokyo, and the only major air base between the Mariannas and Japan. After Navy air attacks in July, Iwo Jima on 10 August was hit for the first time by the 7th AF, which since then has bombed it almost daily. A 7th AF Intelligence officer comments, "If our B-24s were on Iwo Jima, they could blast Hirohito himself, and the Japs know it. On no other islands has there been such concerted effort to repair bomb damage. Since 1891, bats and Japs have been the only animals of any size on Iwo Jima. The bats got there first and will undoubtedly remain there last." Between 10 August and 19 September, to take a typical period, 288 sorties were flown over Iwo Jima and 627.46 tons dropped. Result: Iwo Jima is no longer an effective base.

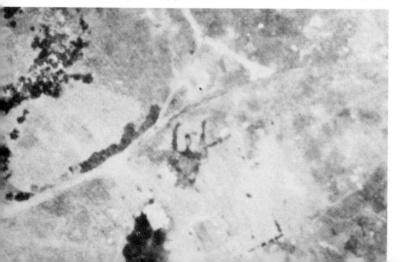

RADIO STATION was not only off the air but almost off the earth after bombing attack (below). B-24s met moderate but consistent fighter opposition from Iwo Jima's two airfields.

FUEL TANKS, storage area, and Jap planes north of Airfield No. 1 presented this tempting target for 7th AF bombs. Below: after attacks the same area is almost entirely obliterated.

BALL NOSE TURRET IS SET UP IN B-24 WITH CANVAS BAG FOR EMPTY CASES AND LINKS UNDERNEATH

B-24 GETS NEW NOSE

Future B-24s will have an Emerson 128 ball nose turret that will reduce maximum weight, provide better visibility for bombardier and navigator, and improve the plane aerodynamically. As a result of tests at Eglin field and recommendations by the AAF Board, first installations will be in airplanes going into production early in 1945.

During the recent tests at Eglin, several Liberators were rigged up with various nose-armament fixtures. One even had a B-17 nose built into it. The tests demonstrated the superiority of the Emerson 128 ball turret, electrically driven and mounting two .50 BAM guns, in the nose position of a B-24G. The cone of fire is 120°, and while this is slightly less than the present radius, it is regarded as sufficient. The gunner's field of view from the new turret is considered satisfactory, and he has room to wear winter flying equipment without discomfort.

An automatic centering device has been developed in the Emerson 128 which enables the pilot or co-pilot to return the turret to center position if gunner is injured. The gunner may then be removed and the guns fired by pilot or co-pilot.

The new armament reduces the weight of the plane by about 225 pounds. The ball turret increases navigator and bombardier visibility by making possible the new side windows seen in the picture above. The new nose turret contributes to better flight performance because it is aerodynamically cleaner than the older style A6B and A15 nose armament; its smooth curve permits better airflow around the nose, and there is no turbulence at the juncture of nose and fuselage, removing the necessity for bulkheads behind turrets. Normal cruising speed of the bomber is stepped up 10 miles per hour.

HEAD-ON VIEW shows flat-head screws which replace round type, cut down friction wear on felt-covered rubber wind seals.

1. **DIVING DOWN** in a coordinated attack on a B-29 are two Jap Tojos at Anshan, Manchuria. Here one Tojo coming in from two o'clock high and another from eleven o'clock high open fire simultaneously from approximately 1,000 yards.

2. **TOJOS CLOSE IN** to 300 yards, firing all the way. Ten per cent of the Jap attacks on this mission were coordinated, more than on all previous missions.

3. **BREAKAWAY** of Tojos is by sharp power dives, as B-29 continues on undamaged. On this mission most of the Jap attacks came from high frontal positions.

Superforts vs. Nips

With the 20th Bomber Command's B-29s becoming seasoned veterans, one thing is obvious: Jap fighters have as yet found no really effective method of attack. On the 21 August mission to Yawata, first time the Superforts met major opposition, 50-60 enemy fighters attacked from all directions with a low, frontal approach preferred. Only 72 per cent of the passes resulted in Jap gunfire, showing that Jap pilots were misjudging the B-29s' high speed and being thrown off by the bombers' evasive tactics. One B-29 was destroyed apparently by an air-to-air bomb, two more in a three-way collision with a Jap.

On the 8 September Anshan mission, and those subsequent, no B-29s are known to have been lost to enemy fighters. The two model sequences shown here are based on engagements during the 26 September Anshan mission in which an increase in coordinated and *high* frontal attacks was reported. On this mission, the enemy was able to fire in only 52 per cent of his passes.

1. **ANOTHER TYPE** of coordinated attack was by two Tojos, which are seen attacking from two o'clock low in trail.

The enemy pilots opened fire at 800 yards, the B-29 returned fire, but Jap planes failed to show any evidence of damage.

2. **ATTACKS PRESSED** to 50 yards by bold Japs, scored hits on the B-29 fuselage behind the radio operator's position.

3. **AS B-29 FIRES,** Tojos go into fast diving turn. The Japs make good use of cloud banks in many of their breakaways.

DRAMATIC RESCUE METHOD TESTED

An agent who has been casing enemy positions on the ground in a Baltic forest or Pacific jungle keeps a rendezvous with a plane in a cleared space. A kit is dropped to him and he takes two telescopic poles out of it and sets them up, stringing a nylon loop between the tops. He snaps his special back-type chute harness to this loop and sits down, curling up like a hedgehog.

This man is now ready to be lifted into a plane by a new AAF technique for rescuing agents, prisoners, and stranded fliers. These photographs were taken during recent tests of the technique in this country.

The plane comes in for contact at 130 mph. Ten feet below and behind the wheels it trails a hook at the end of a wooden pole. This pole guides the tow-rope hook into the pick-up loop. The hook mechanism latches to the pick-up loop and then swings free of the guide pole on its elastic nylon rope, drawing the new passenger skyward as the plane pulls up at 35° angle. Two minutes and 45 seconds later, an electric winch has hauled him into the plane.

AWAITING HOIST on 7 October 1944 is Pvt. Constantine Stiakatis. Pilot of plane was Lt. Norman S. Benedict. Electric winch in plane that plays out elastic rope according to pressure, reduces "g" force on the man being raised.

HE'S OFF, and no bouncing. Stiakatis was "guinea pig" in most recent of four tests with human beings. Weighted dummies and sheep were tried first. Ground observer says: "Subject at takeoff looks as though some strong man had suddenly lifted him in a chair four feet straight off the ground. Then suddenly he sails away and upward much as a glider does."

LEG STRAPS are still fastened. In a moment Stiakatis will undo them, wave arms and legs to reassure onlookers.

PREVIOUS TEST shows S/Sgt. H. C. Conway being reeled up to C-64. IMPACT cover photo shows earlier phase of Conway's test, at exact moment plane hooked into pick-up loop and a split-second before he was pulled upward.

CONWAY SHINNIES up guide pole, through slipstream, to plane. J-edged blades in front of fixed landing gear cut loop if plane is too low on pick-up, so plane's landing gear cannot get tangled in loop and cause injury to man waiting.

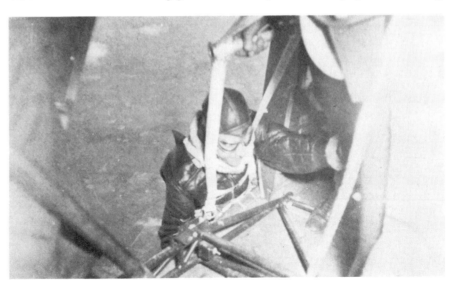

INTO PLANE at last, Conway is unhurt, unjarred, like other four human pick-ups. Project has been developed chiefly by Equipment Laboratory, ATSC, Wright Field, assisted by Aero Medical Lab., Parachute and Glider Branches.

NIGHT ATTACK ON U-BOAT

Dropping flares, an RAF Coastal Command plane, attacks a German sub from 75 feet. Depth charge can be seen exploding near the center of the picture.

IMPACT

ZEKE POKES AT 14th AF
B-24s OVER HONG KONG
See p. 10

DISTRIBUTION
SQUADRONS

OFFICE OF THE
ASSISTANT CHIEF OF AIR STAFF, INTELLIGENCE
WASHINGTON, D. C.

Vol. 2   No. 12
DECEMBER, 1944

BALIKPAPAN—PLOESTI OF THE EAST INDIES, see p. 15

IMPACT
Contents
December, 1944

Confidential

During fire bomb attack on Isle de Cezembre near St. Malo on 31 August, a tactical reconnaissance plane of the 9th AF skims above towering smoke columns which indicate hits. Note fiery burst from bomb dropped by P-38, top, right.

FIRE BOMBS

Napalm fire bombs, first used in active combat in July, are now a standard and very successful AAF weapon in both European and Pacific theaters. Shown here are some of the most effective photographs yet obtained of fire bombs in action near St. Malo. (As discussed in IMPACT, Vol. II, No. 9, this bomb is simply a belly tank loaded with standard QM gasoline thickened with napalm jell, and equipped with an igniting mechanism.)

Fire bombs first hit St. Malo on 17 August. From the 9th AF, 36 P-38s, carrying two 165-gallon capacity tanks on each plane, were dispatched to attack the German-held citadel where Colonel von Aulock, "The Madman of St. Malo," tried to establish permanent residence. The Group Leader had just dropped his bombs, when the ground controller sent word that the citadel had surrendered, so the rest of the Group bombed the secondary target, the Isle de Cezembre. This small, heavily fortified island commanded the deep water channel to St. Malo.

Cezembre got its second baptism of napalm on 31 August (above), although meanwhile it had been hit by HE bombs dropped by B-26s of the 9th AF, and shelled by artillery from ship and shore. This time 56 P-38s did the job, and on the next day the island surrendered.

They Helped Blast Germans from the Isle de Cezembre guarding St. Malo

Investigation revealed that the island was provided with a series of underground shelters, magazine, command post, and control points. Dug into the rock, these were lined in some cases with reinforced concrete. They resisted penetration and there was no evidence of damage to walls or contents by HE bombs. The contents of one shelter were burnt out by napalm seeping through. About 300 prisoners were taken. They told their captors that the combined effect of the bombing was terrifying, especially the napalm. When the napalm invaded the shelter, they made no attempt to put out the fire, but evacuated. Every means of defense larger than machine guns was completely destroyed, and the island could easily have been taken by a landing party.

A report from the theater states, "It is felt that the Fire Bomb accomplished a certain definite portion of damage to personnel, equipment, and morale that was not accomplished by the use of HE. It is not to be construed, however, that this indicates the Fire Bomb would have accomplished this alone. Experience indicates that the Fire Bomb has a definite place when used in conjunction with HE, or on rubble and damage that is a result of HE bombing."

At right, sequence of four pictures shows development of napalm hit on Cezembre, 31 August. Note P-38 in top view.

Continued on page 4

Cezembre is a Dead Duck after Attacks

These two pictures show how Cezembre looked after combined AAF attacks. Above, still smoking from a napalm attack, is the crater-covered island, lying two miles off Dinard. At right is all that remains of one of six old, large French guns that were Cezembre's main defense. The other five were also destroyed. There were said, too, to be three AA guns. The mount of one was found in the valley. Apparently the Germans depended on these and on machine guns for defense against landing, as the big guns probably could not be depressed enough to cover a landing. There seemed to be no demolition of guns—it being hardly necessary, though the Germans did destroy papers, radio, stores.

Confidential

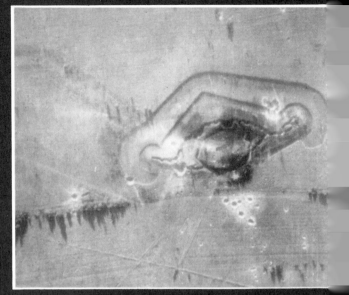

Fire bombs dropped by 9th AF P-47s on 28 September sear bomb-scarred Metz fort. Right, after strike.

Forts on Siegfried Line, 50 miles east of Metz, are bombed on 9 October by B-26s. Right, after strike.

METZ

How 9th AF fighter-bombers and bombers worked in close cooperation with General Patton's troops pushing towards Metz is shown above. These fortified positions have seen many sieges. Fortified by Romans, sacked by Attila, rebuilt for Louis XIV, and for Napoleon III, they now have been battered by a potent combination of napalm and HE bombs, and are falling one by one to U. S. forces.

IN THE WAKE OF

"The enemy has succeeded, by concentrated and ceaseless attacks from the air, in disorganizing our supply to such an extent and to cause such losses of railway rolling stock and vehicles that supply has become a serious problem."

In a memorandum to his troops last June, Field Marshal von Rundstedt, German commander-in-chief in the West, thus described the tremendously effective role that fighter-bombers play in isolation of a battlefield. The pictures from France on these two pages are further evidence of the great work that has been and is being performed by 8th, 9th, 12th and 15th AF fighter-bombers.

Aftermath of the attack at Gisors 18 Aug., shown at left and below, on a German troop train, is a classic example of effective dive bombing and strafing. Here the target was protected by a deep curving cut through a hill and in addition was well camouflaged by a thick covering of branches and straw. Yet all bombs were accurately

German troop train met five 8th AF P-47s on curve at Gisors, France.

Camouflage with branches didn't fool P-47 pilots.

Searchlights on the train were demolished also.

Ten 500-lb. bombs and fancy strafing did the job.

Fire completed devastation after fighters departed.

FIGHTER ATTACKS

placed; strafing only polished off the job.

Imagine 400 Hun fighters racing up and down the Pennsylvania Railroad between Trenton and Philadelphia, completely unopposed by U. S. interceptors, and shooting up everything in sight. On 24 Oct. P-47s and P-51s of the 8th AF did just exactly this in the Brunswick-Hanover area when they beat up 150 locomotives, destroying 61, and in addition accounted for 346 railway cars destroyed and 119 damaged. In another dissection of the German rail system, on 9 Nov. near Saarbrucken 8th AF Mustangs knocked off 61 more locomotives and 227 railroad cars of the rapidly dwindling Nazi supply.

Fighter-bombing is highly dangerous due to the accuracy and concentration of German automatic weapons and small-arms fire. Losses are not light. Therefore, the achievement of pilots who must pound in there at low level day after day, certain they'll be shot at, is a truly heroic one.

8th AF P-38 strafers blew munitions train off face of the earth here.

Marshaling yard at Compiegne, France, was of small value to the Germans after visit by 8th AF P-47s.

CHINA AIR BASE RETREAT

The vigorous Japanese advance through Hunan and Kwangsi provinces which began last spring and inexorably keeps pushing the Chinese armies back, has compelled the 14th AF to demolish and evacuate several of its important bases in that region. Fighters and bombers carry on with their missions as the installations are being destroyed: the planes land by the glare of burning buildings, take off through rolling black smoke, and fly over roads choked with refugees for one more thrust at the Jap lines before the final retreat to another base. Airstrips are blown up last.

This has been the story at station after station: it began with Hengyang and Lingling last summer, continued with Kweilin and Tanchuk early in the fall, and with Liuchow in November. Photos on this page show destruction of installations at two of the three Kweilin airfields in mid-September (the third remained in use till the Japs crowded painfully close in October). On the opposite page is an unusually graphic picture of Tanchuk after it was evacuated.

Good earth is gouged deep by 1,000-lb. G.P. bomb.

Above, Chinese prepare to bury bomb in runway.

Incendiary bullet is fired at gas drum inside building.

Kweilin hostel after incendiary bullet treatment.

Tanchuk air base, West river, Kwangsi Province, photographed by 21st Photo Reconnaissance Squadron after 14th AF evacuated airfield in September. Following ground demolition process, base was bombed by departing planes.

SHIPS BURNING

Smoke pours from Kowloon docks and Jap shipping burns in Hong Kong harbor during 16 Oct. attack by 14th AF.

14th HITS HONG KONG AND JAP BRIDGES

Japanese merchant ships were crowded into Hong Kong harbor on 16 October, a time when the waters of the South China sea were too hot for the comfort of enemy vessels. Then the 14th AF suddenly made Hong Kong harbor hot: 28 B-24s and 12 B-25s came roaring in to bomb Jap shipping and the great Kowloon docks.

The picture above, like the one on IMPACT'S cover and the three at the top of the next page, testify to the success of the attack. The Kowloon docks are among the largest in any part of the Pacific, and those selected for the 16 October mission (on the smoking peninsular spur in the photo above) consist of three drydocks with respective dimensions of 680′ x 90′, 435′ x 60′ and 265′ x 40′, two repair slips 225′ x 30′, four building ways 450′, launching slip 175′ x 25′, six cranes, and miscellaneous buildings. These drydocks can be used for all types of repair and refitting, and for the building of ships up to 10,000 tons. The

Liberators dropped 294 x 500-pound G.P. bombs from 17,000 feet, 77 percent of them in the target area (see photos at top of next page). The B-25s came in at low level and hit the harbor shipping (observe boats on fire in picture above). Two vessels confirmed as sunk totalled approximately 8,600 tons, while eleven more ships visibly damaged represented some 40,000 additional tons. These figures do not include the dock area, where bombs sent a 270′ ship under water and probably damaged several others, among them three 190′ ships. Thirty-five fighters, P-40s and P-51s, served as escort and met with little opposition.

The 14th again effectively attacked Kowloon docks several times in November, and has continued to hammer Jap targets at widely dispersed points on the Asiatic mainland. The two pictures at the bottom of the next page show attacks in French Indo-China, where the 14th has repeatedly cut the vital railroad line from Saigon to the north.

Confidential

270' SHIP SUNK
BY DIRECT HITS

NEAR MISSES ON 420'
PASSENGER CARGO SHIP

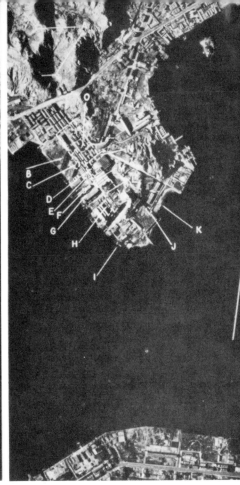

Kowloon attack effectiveness is revealed in three photos above. First shows strike on 16 October. Second is an earlier picture with bomb plot overlaid subsequent to the attack. Third picture, made on 17 October reconnaissance, indicates damage as follows: (a) no damage by 10 bombs 2,000′ off target, (b) probable damage to 400′ vessel in westernmost drydock, (c) middle section of pattern shop smashed, (d) pattern shop building almost totally destroyed, (e) direct hit on east end of boiler shop, (f) middle part of storage building nicked, (g) probable damage to 175′ vessel in drydock, (h) machine shop slightly damaged, (i) 270′ cargo vessel sunk beneath crane, (j) 35′ section of wall knocked out, (k) probable damage to 280′ beached hulk, (l) blacksmith shop hit and forge shop destroyed, (m) corner of pattern shop crushed, (n) direct hit on west end of foundry, (o) several buildings destroyed in the barracks area.

Railroad bridge over Dai Giang river in northern French Indo-China is neatly pinpointed by 14th AF Liberators.

Three Libs of 14th AF, bombing at 200 ft., destroyed one pier of bridge on 8 Sept. attack at Hué, French Indo-China.

Captured Oscar MK. II

No matter how much Allied fighter pilots learn from actual combat, they gain an even greater advantage over the enemy if they have the opportunity to fly captured pursuit planes in mock combat trials against our front-line fighters. In the model sequences shown on these pages it is possible to observe some of the results of preliminary combat trials flown in Australia between the type 1 F Oscar 2A and a P-47D-23. *(Distances between planes in these photos have been reduced because of space limitations. Results of the maneuvers demonstrated were essentially the same at altitudes of 10,000 feet and below.)*

The trials were made at 5,000′, 10,000′, and 20,000′. The Oscar was flown by Lt. C. F. Whistler, and the P-47 at altitudes of 5,000′ and 10,000′ was flown by Lt. A. V. Jackson who has had experience with Japanese fighters. Lt. W. H. Strand, with 450 combat hours in P-47s and experience against Jap pilots, flew the Thunderbolt at 20,000′.

Of the trials Lt. Whistler, pilot of the Oscar, reports:

"On takeoff I got 38″ Hg. and 2,600 rpm with the prop control a little back of full forward. The fuel pressure flickered back and forth as it always does on takeoff. It had little tendency to swing to the left and was easy to correct with slight rudder pressure.

"At both 5,000′ and 10,000′ I pulled up in a hammerhead stall and the set-up was the same for both altitudes. The airspeed was below 50 mph at the time I fell off to the right and the P-47 overran me and I could drop on his tail for a short burst before he could dive away.

"At 10,000′ I intended to loop at about 190 but I kept waiting for the P-47 to close up until I was doing 240 mph in a slight dive before I started my loop. I came out doing about 200 mph within firing range of the P-47. If he had not followed me so far into the loop, I think he could have been out of range before I completed the loop."

Of the same maneuver the P-47 pilot, Lt. Jackson, says:

"If the P-47 pulled up firing until 200 mph was reached,

1. **Oscar pulls up** into a hammerhead stall from 190 IAS while P-47 holds him in sights long enough to hit him.

2. **P-47 overruns** Oscar as Jap plane's airspeed falls off to 50 mph. Thunderbolt kicks off to right to regain speed.

3. **Complete advantage** then is held by Oscar as he drops onto P-47's tail to get in burst before making breakaway.

1. **Oscar loops** at 240 mph, P-47's cruising speed. Thunderbolt pulls into vertical stall, unable to follow through.

is Flown against P-47D

then dropped its nose and ran away, it could be away from Oscar before he could pull up into a firing position within range. In the P-47's loop it pulled away on the dive and looped far above the Oscar. It seemed that the Oscar could not follow in the large arc of the P-47's loop."

Characteristic of almost all Jap pursuit planes, the Oscar has a terrifically sharp rate of turn at low and medium altitudes. Lt. Whistler states, "The P-47 could fire at me but would have a big deflection shot. On the second pass by the P-47 I turned to the right. My turn didn't seem as tight as ones to the left, but the Oscar's advantage is as good in the right turn as it is to the left. My airspeed dropped off to about 140 mph during these turning maneuvers."

Discussing the same tight turns at 20,000' the Oscar pilot says that at an IAS of 175 he started a steep turn to the left with the P-47 about 250 yards astern. By tightening his turn more as his airspeed dropped, he caused the P-47 to pass the Oscar by the time it had turned only 150°. Lt. Whistler reversed his turn in the Oscar as the P-47 continued to turn, pulled up, and would have barely been able to get in a head-on shot at the Thunderbolt.

Lt. Jackson flew the Oscar at 20,000'. He reports:

"The Oscar and P-47 aren't in the same league at 20,000'. The P-47 with its 230 mph cruising speed, moves rapidly away from the Oscar's 170 at that altitude.

"The Oscar is practically hopeless at 20,000' or above."

Of the trials at 20,000', Lt. Strand, in the P-47, reports that the Thunderbolt is much faster than the Oscar. He recommends use of high IAS on the P-47 in order to gain an altitude advantage over the Oscar, because the P-47 can climb right away from the Jap plane with a shallow rate of climb. At 20,000' the Oscar begins to lose its airspeed, and the P-47 is just beginning to get its maximum qualities. Lt. Strand does not recommend looping the P-47 with an Oscar in combat, because the Jap will complete his loop at such low airspeed that the P-47 cannot follow him through.

1. **Oscar cruises** at 25″ Hg. with 2,050 rpm at 185 IAS as P-47 starts run from 1,000 yds. above and behind.

2. **Diving** slightly to a position about 400 yards behind Oscar, P-47 has Jap plane squarely in sights briefly.

3. **90° of bank** is obtained by Oscar before P-47 can start turn giving only 1½ seconds lead at extreme deflection.

2. **Thunderbolt stalls,** falls forward to recover as Oscar continues around on arc of loop, bores in towards P-47.

3. **Before P-47** can regain speed, Oscar pulls onto his tail within range. P-47's loop has far greater arc and speed.

GORONTALO SURPRISE
5th AF Bombs Celebes Harbor

Typical of the day by day destruction of Jap shipping and shore installations in the N.E.I. is the attack on Gorontalo on the northern neck of the main Celebes island, illustrated here in a sequence of three pictures. The attack was made on 16 September by 14 B-25s escorted by 11 P-38s of the 5th AF. Striking swiftly at low level, the Mitchells achieved complete surprise.

Not a shot was fired from the ground. No enemy planes intercepted. Terrific explosions resulted. The entire area was left in flames which were still burning after midnight with smoke to 9,000 feet and explosions still rocking the area. Targets across the river from the warehouses were further bombed and more fires started during a mission that night by two B-24s and a PBY.

Over Gorontalo warehouses a B-25, followed by another, drops 2 bombs.

Warehouses are left in flames. Below, two of the attackers turn homeward, leaving a smoking Jap tanker.

EAST INDIES OIL

Liberators of 13th and 5th AF fly through inferno caused by 10 October strike on Balikpapan refineries.

OPENING BLOWS ARE AIMED AT A MAJOR SOURCE OF JAP FUEL

In terms of estimated 1944 consumption, the East Indies supply more than 85 percent of Japan's aviation gasoline, and more than 75 percent of her fuel oil.

These figures explain why since 30 September oil targets in the Netherlands East Indies have begun to receive some of the same concentrated AAF hellfire that reduced German liquid fuel output by more than 75 percent in six months.

Japan's need for N.E.I. fuel oil is particularly acute. Total 1944 Jap requirements are estimated at forty million barrels, and the total production is forty-two million. Only ten million are produced in Japan's Inner Zone, the balance coming from the Netherlands East Indies.

"In this tight situation," quoting directly from an August report prepared by AC/AS, Intelligence, "eliminating N.E.I. fuel oil would curtail operations of the Japanese Navy and part of the Japanese merchant fleet. Any serious curtailment of N.E.I. fuel oil could be expected to have direct effects, though such effects would not be critical until there had been a serious curtailment of a fuel oil stockpile currently estimated at eight months' supply."

On the next two pages is an account of the first heavy AAF blows at East Indies petroleum production, aimed at Balikpapan, one of five main N.E.I. production areas and source of an estimated 35 percent of Jap fuel supply.

Ground view of Balikpapan taken in 1940 shows harbor and view over greater part of refinery.

LONGEST B-24 MISSIONS IN SWPA SMASH OIL PLANTS AT BALIKPAPAN

On at least two counts the 13th AF mission against Balikpapan on 30 September was history-making. It was the first heavy strike against strategic Jap targets in the South Pacific. It was the longest SWPA mission—2,500-mile round trip—ever flown by Liberators in formation.

Called the "Ploesti of the East Indies," Balikpapan bears much the same relation to Japan as the great Rumanian oil refinery did to Germany. Balikpapan is Japan's largest refinery in the N.E.I., with a capacity of roughly four million barrels of crude oil. Now it is believed to be the only N.E.I. refinery for lubricating oils, and it supplies much needed aviation gasoline for the Jap air force in the SWPA. Crudes from SE Borneo, Taraban, Boela and East Java are processed here, stored in the big tank farm, or shipped by tankers. Destruction of this plant would have not only an almost immediate effect on Japan's operations in this theater, but would seriously weaken her entire Philippine and Empire defenses.

Balikpapan's main plants *(see far right)* are the Pandansari and Edeleanu refineries, and the paraffin works. These had been bombed before, but the Japs made quick repairs and work continued, evidently under the assumption that their distance from our bases guaranteed immunity from all except token raids.

This assumption proved to be very wrong.

Our concentrated attacks began on 30 September by 69 Liberators of the 13th AF and 90th Bomb Group in the 5th AF. Fighter interception was "vicious," and continued to be so during later missions. We destroyed seven fighters, with nine probables. Eleven of our Libs were holed, and we lost two.

Japs strafed our crews as they bailed out, even engaging one man with a wing tip.

A second strike by 40 Libs on 3 October scored scattered hits on the refineries, and started huge fires. A theater report states, "Arriving over the target, the planes were met by intense AA and no interception. As the ships turned back, 40-odd Zeros fell on the giant bombers like vultures. Seven bombers were shot down by AA and Zeros. Three more dropped out on the long trip home. We downed three Zeros. Our planes were under fire from the time they reached the coast, over the target, and on the way out. Interception lasted over an hour. It is strictly a suicide run."

But during the next two strikes the picture brightened. They varied from the first two strikes in three respects: (1) employment of two bombing altitudes, (2) *use of fighter escort at extreme long range*, and (3) degree of destruction attained. On 10 October three groups of 5th AF B-24s led the attack from 11,000 feet, and two groups of the 13th AF dropped from about 20,000 feet. The Japs dropped aerial phosphorous bombs, as usual, and made the very rare achievement of a direct hit on a Liberator cockpit, causing it to explode in mid air. The strike of 14 October again was led by three 5th AF groups, followed by two from the 13th. How we licked the Jap fighter problem is best told by the figures for these two missions. We destroyed 76 enemy aircraft, and lost five bombers and six fighters of our own. In addition to a good deal of miscellaneous damage, the paraffin and lubricating oil works were crippled, Pandansaru was disabled temporarily, at least, and the Edeleanu refinery was completely knocked out.

Paraffin Refinery, spewing black smoke, was hit by 75 percent of bombs dropped by 13th AF on its successful 10 October strike.

Cracking Plant, secondary target, was hit on 10 October when smoke from paraffin plant hid primary target, Pandansari.

Okayama gets concentrated bombing by B-29s 14 Oct.

B-29 FIELD DAY
Japs Lose Big Formosa Aircraft Plant

At right is blunt proof, if any is needed, that our B-29s now hit hard and heavy. It is the big Jap aircraft assembly, modification, and repair plant at Okayama on Formosa taken a few days after three coordinated attacks: one by the Navy, which concentrated on the aircraft and hangar area, and two on the main plant area by the 20th Bomber Command. These 20th B.C. attacks, closely timed with carrier-based strikes, helped pave the way for the Philippine invasion in mid October.

Following on the heels of the Navy strike, 103 B-29s from the 20th B.C. struck at the big target on 14 October. No fighters intercepted, and we lost no planes to enemy action. A follow-up attack of only 33 planes over the target on 16 October was enough to finish the job. This time about 35 Jap fighters showed up, attacked 26 of our planes, but did not shoot any down. Nine aerial attacks with phosphorus type bombs were made by the enemy without damage to our aircraft. Total tonnage dropped on both missions was about 850 tons of HE and incendiary bombs. Now Okayama's plant, with some million square feet of floor space gutted, is no longer a key unit in enemy operations south of Japan.

At Okayama aircraft plant, 43 out of 80 buildings were destroyed by B-29 attack on 14 October. Two days later, after second attack, only six small buildings remained intact.

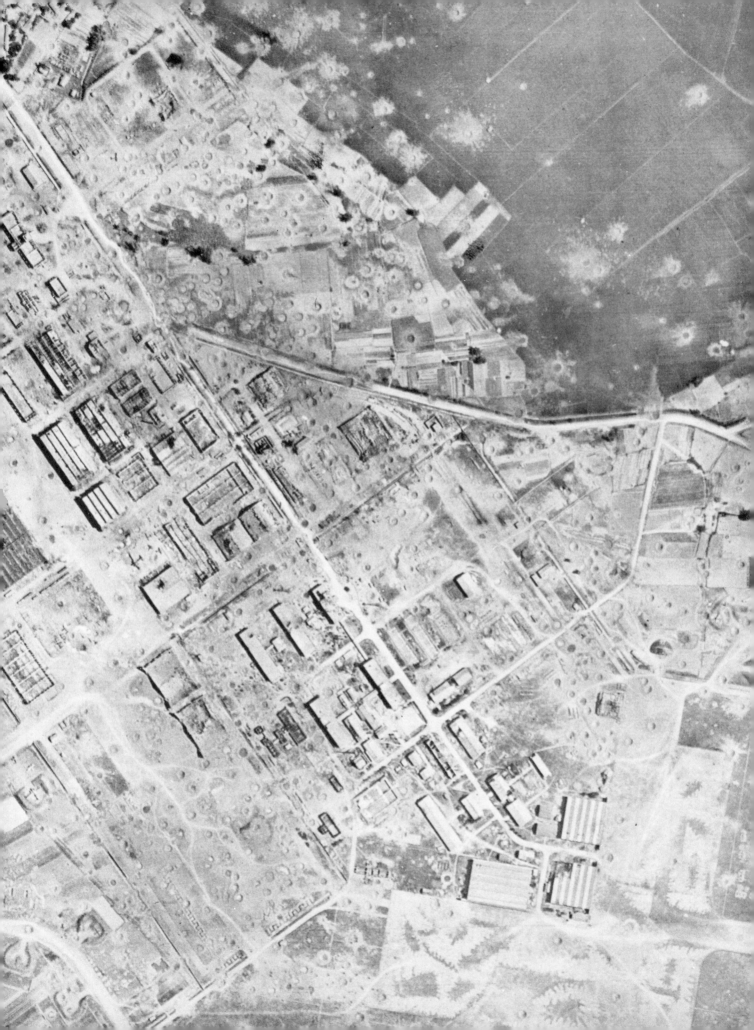

Over Debrecen, Hungary, on 21 Sept., this B-17 received a direct hit by heavy flak during bomb run on military traffic.

ALMOST CUT IN TWO, FORT GETS HOME
Pilot on First Mission Flies It 520 Miles without Controls

"The-Swoose-Cannot-Fly?" was the name of a B-17 famous early in the war. Here are pictures of another Fort, equally deserving of fame, whose name could well be "How-in-Hell-Can-It-Fly?" Yet, fly it did, all the way from Hungary back to its base in Italy where it landed successfully.

In a bit of piloting that would have done a veteran proud, the landing was accomplished by 2nd Lt. G. M. Miller of the 2nd Bomb Gp., on his first mission as first pilot. He had previously flown 22 combat missions as co-pilot. Here is what Maj. Gen. Nathan F. Twining, Commanding 15th AF, says about it:

"While over the target, a direct hit by heavy flak exploded in the waist and almost blew the aircraft apart. One waist gunner and tail gunner were killed, the radio operator and other waist gunner were wounded. As the rudder cables were severed and the elevator controls hopelessly damaged by the explosion, the B-17 immediately went out of control and lost altitude into the clouds. Recovery was effected and flight continued in the clouds to avoid losing further altitude. Directional control was maintained by use of the outboard engines and altitude was controlled by increase or decrease of engine power.

"Lt. Miller flew the B-17 520 miles over enemy territory and across the Adriatic sea to its home field. While coming in for a landing, an engine began to cut out at an altitude of 300 feet, but Lt. Miller managed to retain control and a perfect landing was made on a crash strip beside the runway. In spite of a smooth touchdown, the fuselage crumpled and fell apart at the waist before No. 38078 could be brought to a stop and taxied to its position on the line.

"This is an outstanding example, not only of the ability of our heavy bombers to withstand battle damage, but also of the skill and presence of mind of our air crews in carrying through their missions to a successful conclusion in the face of opposition, casualties, and difficulties in the air."

Incredible damage is seen below, at left.

This One Got Back, Too

A direct hit by flak clipped off the nose of this 8th AF B-17 over Cologne, Germany, on 15 October, killing the bombardier. The pilot's account follows:

"As soon as I recovered from the shock of the explosion I found all four engines running and flight controls operating satisfactorily. Numbers 2 and 3 props were hitting the dangling nose guns, but this soon ceased.

"Upon making our base, because of damage, I made a high approach, power on with partial flaps. This killed excess airspeed, making it possible to land reasonably short. I applied brakes when speed had slowed sufficiently and when the brakes did quit, we stopped safely just off runway."

AAF COMES UP WITH SINGLE-TAIL B-24

XB-24N is Lighter, Has Improved Stability and New Armament

A close look at the pictures on these two pages will show you that the B-24N, going into production early in 1945, is not just an old-type Liberator with a new tail, but an entirely redesigned airplane. With the new features, the AAF expects to increase operational performance by a reduction of weight and drag. Pilot, navigator, and bombardier will have far better visibility, an additional 600 horse power will be available for take-off, and armament revisions will greatly improve effectiveness of the plane's fire power.

This aircraft is the result of three years of experimenting with variations of the Liberator. It has long been realized that the twin-fin empennage lacks sufficient directional stability in the event of power failure on one side. After numerous tests, a satisfactory single-fin tail assembly was developed. A variation of this was adapted by the Navy for the PB4-Y2.

The major design changes in the B-24N incorporate the Emerson 128 nose turret (shown in last month's IMPACT), the model A-3F lightweight upper turret, and a lightweight version of the Motor Products -5 tail turret. The plane will also probably utilize one of several proposed barbette gun mounts, designed to replace the lower ball turret and the hand-held waist gun. The Motor Products proposal illustrated in the lower right hand picture on the opposite page consists of hydraulically operated, remotely controlled barbettes; the gunner's sighting station (also shown in the photo) is located at the present waist-gun position. The installation, which would reduce the drag and effect a saving in weight of approximately 700 pounds, covers the fields of fire now in the range of the guns to be replaced.

The R1830-75 engines provide 150 additional horse power apiece and, with the turbo flight hoods, should account for a definite increase in speed and operational ceiling, plus a greater margin of safety on the take-off. Simplified communications equipment will reduce the over-all weight about 200 pounds. A thermal de-icing system for wings and empennage also provides cabin heat. The instrument panel and control pedestal have been completely redesigned, and the pilot's canopy has bullet-resisting glass in the windshield. There are emergency escape hatches for pilot and co-pilot and another over the rear bomb bay.

Oblique shows the current type B-24J

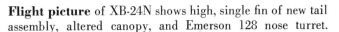

Flight picture of XB-24N shows high, single fin of new tail assembly, altered canopy, and Emerson 128 nose turret.

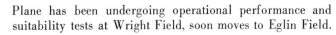

Plane has been undergoing operational performance and suitability tests at Wright Field, soon moves to Eglin Field.

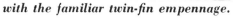
with the familiar twin-fin empennage.

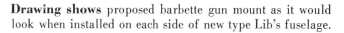
New XB-24N stands by for contrast with J-type Liberator at the left.

Tail view of XB-24N shows Bell power-boost mount which will be replaced by lightweight Motor Products -5 tail turret.

Drawing shows proposed barbette gun mount as it would look when installed on each side of new type Lib's fuselage.

V-2

From the day that Allied Intelligence first began to fit together bits of information about the monster German rocket which was to level London, the truth about V-2 has persistently proved more fantastic than the rumors. It has grown in size from a supposed twenty-odd feet to a confirmed 45 feet 10 inches. Its maximum velocity is now known to exceed 3.500 miles an hour. It soars to a height of 58 miles into the lofty calm of the ionosphere, and it can be launched practically anywhere.

The huge sites in the Pas de Calais (IMPACT, Vol. II, No. 9) are now known not to be connected with launching. The typical launching site proves to be nothing more than a widened spot in a road large enough to park a few trucks. A permanent concrete slab is imbedded here, and the rocket brought up on a large dolly which upends it on a low firing table placed on the slab. After lengthy computations and adjustments, the rocket is filled with fuel, and its instruments checked. Everybody then departs to a safe distance and it is started up. wobbling slowly into the air trailing a cloud of smoke.

Although it contains radio equipment, this is believed to be for the purpose of monitoring gyros, which control the flight of the rocket along a preselected trajectory, after it has gathered sufficient speed to fly a true course.

Rocket is launched after being placed in vertical position (left) on firing block and fueled up from tank trucks containing liquid oxygen and alcohol (main fuels) and hydrogen peroxide (fuel for driving turbines).

Continued on next page

V-2 craters average 35 ft. across, 15 ft. deep, but are sometimes 75 by 30 ft. as pictured above and below. Terrific speed at impact causes this.

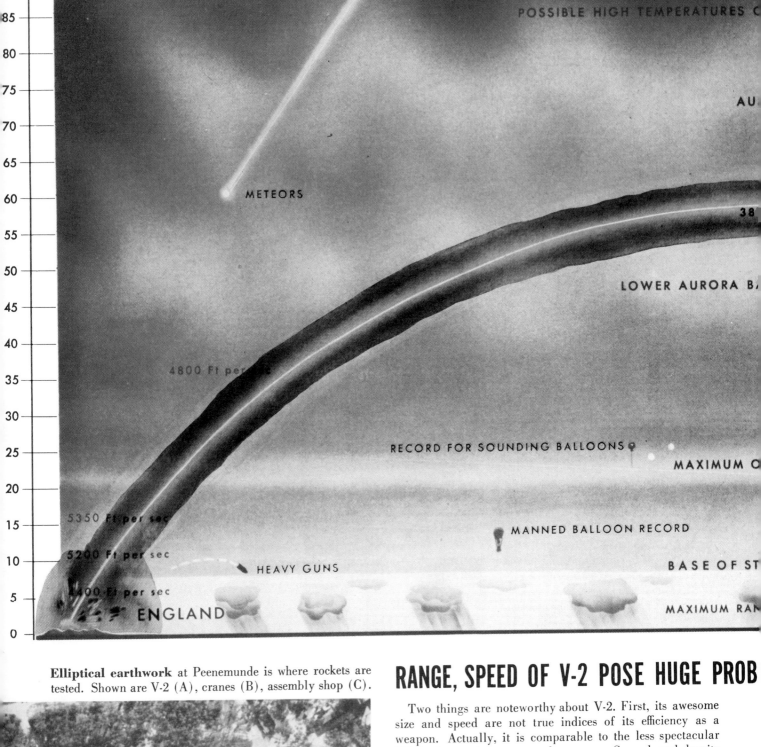

V-2 TRAJECTORY

HEIGHT IN MILES

90
85
80
75
70
65
60
55
50
45
40
35
30
25
20
15
10
5
0

POSSIBLE HIGH TEMPERATURES C

AU

38

METEORS

LOWER AURORA BA

4800 Ft per sec

RECORD FOR SOUNDING BALLOONS

MAXIMUM O

MANNED BALLOON RECORD

5350 Ft per sec

5200 Ft per sec

BASE OF ST

400 Ft per sec

HEAVY GUNS

ENGLAND

MAXIMUM RA

Elliptical earthwork at Peenemunde is where rockets are tested. Shown are V-2 (A), cranes (B), assembly shop (C).

RANGE, SPEED OF V-2 POSE HUGE PROB

Two things are noteworthy about V-2. First, its awesome size and speed are not true indices of its efficiency as a weapon. Actually, it is comparable to the less spectacular V-1 in destructive power and accuracy. Second, and despite the foregoing, it should not be overlooked that V-2 is a bold and brilliant engineering experiment. Never has man fired a projectile so far, or so fast, or so high. The construction problems alone are formidable, considering the enormous stresses and changes in temperature encountered during flight. Range and directional control are even more complicated. Consider the following. V-2 takes off in an uneasy wobble, quickly gathers momentum, and at the end of burning is traveling about one mile a second. Shortly after launching, it is deflected from its vertical course either

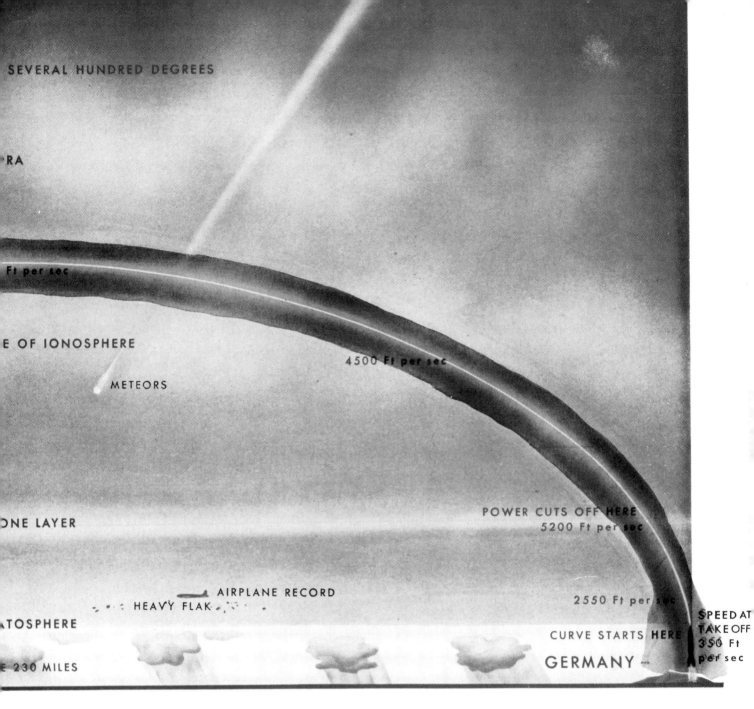

SEVERAL HUNDRED DEGREES

RA

Ft per sec

E OF IONOSPHERE

4500 Ft per sec

METEORS

POWER CUTS OFF HERE
5200 Ft per sec

ONE LAYER

AIRPLANE RECORD

HEAVY FLAK

2550 Ft per sec

TOSPHERE

CURVE STARTS HERE

SPEED AT
TAKE OFF
350 Ft
per sec

E 230 MILES

GERMANY

LEMS IN CONSTRUCTION AND CONTROL

Earthwork was hit by 8th AF on 4 August and heavily damaged. Similar works also exist at Friedrichshaven.

by remote control or preset gyro. All this time its weight decreases steadily because of fuel consumption. After power ceases, gravity takes over, and from this point to target, the course is that of a free projectile in space, affected, however, by the rotation of the earth, and by the great differences in air density at different altitudes. At the top of its flight curve speed is reduced (from 5,200 feet per second at the point of power cutoff) to 3,850. Gravity pull during the swoop groundward gradually increases the speed again until a maximum of 5,350 feet per second is reached. By this time the projectile is again traveling through dense atmosphere. It decelerates rapidly during the last fifteen miles of flight, to an approximate 3,000 feet per second on impact, the nose becoming red hot through skin friction.

Extreme accuracy of paratroop drop at Groesbeek, Holland, is aided by compact, flat formations of 9th T.C.C.

CG-4As of the 9th T.C.C. swoop in for landings on the broad flatlands of Holland near Nijmegen. In first five days despite weather American C-47s and gliders delivered 27,419 combat troops and 4,086,235 lbs. of equipment, including 9,385 gallons of gasoline. In contrast to Normandy glider landings, few losses occurred because of terrain hazards.

American paratroopers land west of Grave, Holland, and rush into action to seize key bridge across Maas river.

Holland: Proving Ground for Airborne Operations

The September invasion of Holland, largest in the history of airborne warfare, proved conclusively that daylight paratroop and glider operations over heavily defended enemy positions can be a brilliant success.

For the period D-Day (17 September) to D plus 9 (26 September) British and American troop-carrier pilots flew 5,292 sorties and towed 2,602 gliders into action. Successfully delivered were 39,620 troops and 4,595 tons of military supplies at a cost of only 2.3 percent loss in aircraft.

Great dividends from daylight were gained in the accuracy of paratroop drops, in landing of gliders, and in rapid assembly of troops. Battalion commanders of the 82nd and 101st Airborne Divisions have described operations as the best in the history of their units.

Three factors are responsible for the tremendous success of the operation, despite powerful German defenses:

1. Overwhelming attack air forces knocked out many flak positions before and during airborne operations and protected troop carriers from enemy fighters.

2. Maximum of tactical surprise was attained through able staff work; large forces were placed in a minimum of time and simultaneously.

3. Thorough training of troop carrier and airborne personnel produced almost perfect landings.

American airborne troops captured intact the Maas bridge at Grave, two bridges over the Maas-Waal Canal, high ground between Groesbeek and Nijmegen, the cities of Eindhoven, Beek and Nijmegen, and most important of all, the famous Rhine bridge at Nijmegen. The whole operation, despite the withdrawal of British airborne troops at Arnhem in the face of overwhelming odds of enemy troops and fire power, has been judged highly successful.

Continued on next page

Air Resupply Vital

Air resupply proved absolutely essential in the airborne invasion of Holland. Major General James M. Gavin, Commanding 82nd Airborne Division, reports that even though contact was established by his men with English troops soon after landing, the British did not have necessary supplies available.

The B-24 resupply mission on D plus 1 was the only one flown at proper altitude, due to weather and enemy flak. Considerable dispersion occurred because of variance from release points, but the resupply drop served its purpose even though 20 percent of the equipment fell into enemy hands.

Resupply missions on other days were not so successful, not only because of bad weather but because enemy ground opposition grew more severe once the surprise element was over, as was expected.

Gen. Gavin says, "Parachute resupply is, at its very best, an emergency means of resupply, and I believe to function properly it would require

Upper picture shows flak-damaged C-47 plunging to earth during landing of 1st Allied Airborne Army. Below, crashed transport burns after crew bailed out.

8th AF B-24s drop equipment on D plus 1 to airborne troops in Holland. Mission successfully released 782

in Airborne Attack

about one third of the combat force engaged being used as recovery detail. This is impossible in hard fought situations such as existed in Holland. Troop carrier command pilots made every effort to effect resupply despite enemy interference; and I believe that supplies delivered were an essential contribution to the 82nd's combat success. It is hoped that in future training the problems of resupply missions will be worked out in practice."

Pilots in the CBI theater, though not so accustomed to working with paratroops as T.C.C. units of the ETO, are far more familiar with air resupply problems. Benefits of their experience will be utilized in training in the United States before T.C. units leave for overseas.

In a tribute to the 9th T.C.C. Gen. Gavin says, "The 82nd could not have successfully accomplished any of its missions but for courageous performance of the pilots, which has been the subject of boundless favorable comment by all ground personnel."

American paratroopers plough through fire from German 88s in assault on Arnhem. Flak prior to landings caused few casualties among airborne personnel.

tons of supplies at cost of 16 Liberators.

Dirt and flame spurt as flak-damaged 8th AF B-24 plows into Holland field.

A-26 INVADER MAKES OPERATIONAL DEBUT

Another problem has recently been added to the Luftwaffe's mounting collection of troubles: the A-26 Invader is in combat in the ETO.

Scheduled to replace the B-26 and A-20 as the AAF's principal medium level air weapon, between 6 September and 19 September A-26s successfully flew eight missions over Europe. Targets were heavy gun positions at Brest, the Bath Dike (a rail and road causeway) in Holland, marshaling yards at Duren, Germany, and German defense positions at Nancy and Metz.

The Invader is probably the best medium bomber or attack airplane in the world today. Combat cruising speed of 220-230 IAS, as employed in the ETO, gives maximum range and most efficient performance. To maintain this speed, the A-26 pulls 28" to 34" hg. of manifold pressure with 2,050 to 2,100 rpm's for loads up to 4,000 lbs. The same cruising power settings with normal bomb load give a rate of climb of 400 to 500 ft. per minute at 190 IAS and 205 mph on bomb run with doors open. A constant power setting can be used for climbing, cruising, and bombing.

Radius of action with the formation shown at right and used in the ETO is 450 miles, still maintaining the necessary fuel reserve. Roughly, this gives the A-26 an increase of 75 miles in range over a Marauder and 100 miles over a Havoc. Fuel consumption has been lower than expected, averaging 156½ gals./hr. for the eight missions.

Experience shows that 12,000 feet is the best possible operational altitude for medium level bombardment with the A-26. No low level missions have yet been reported over Germany. In other theaters where the risk from flak is not as great as it is over Germany, the speed and maneuverability of the A-26 will make it highly adaptable to low level bombing and strafing attacks.

To date the Invaders have met no enemy fighter opposition and have encountered flak on only two missions with minor damage. Single engine performance is unquestionably the best of any bomber in operation today.

Potent one-two punch of 75 mm and 37 mm cannon in interchangeable attack nose of A-26 Invader can knock out enemy fortifications and gun positions.

New bubble canopy and raised cockpit of A-26 permits greater visibility.

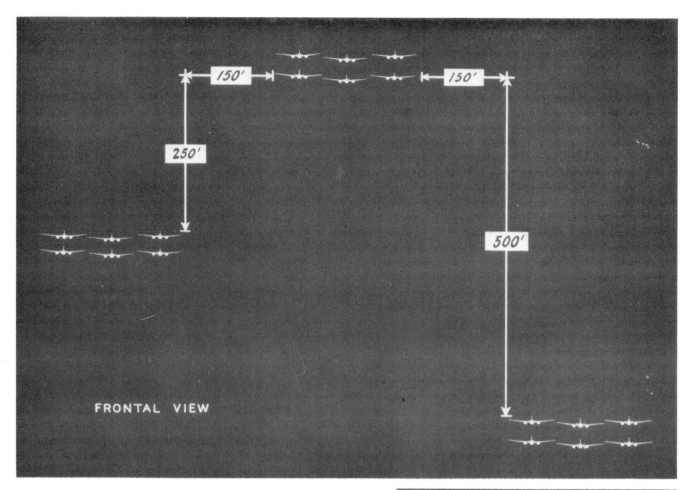

FRONTAL VIEW

Frontal view of A-26 combat formation shows relative positions of the boxes. Wing men fly level with or slightly above lead airplane so that wing tips just clear. Formation is much similiar to that flown by A-20s and B-26s in ETO. No. 2 flight flies 150 feet to the right and 250 feet below lead; No. 3 flight 150 feet to left and 500 feet below.

Side view of Invaders' combat box shows only four out of six planes of squadron because wing men are on the same level. Noses of wing men just clear the tail of lead plane in each element. Second element lead plane flies 20 feet back and 20 feet down. No. 2 flight flies 250 feet below to the right, No. 3 flight 500 feet below to the left.

Plan view—Compactness of formation is easily visible from this angle. No. 2 flight flies 150 feet to right with lead plane opposite tail of first flight. No. 3 flight occupies same position on left, though flights do exchange positions. Formation is highly flexible and well suited for extreme speeds and maneuverability of Invader.

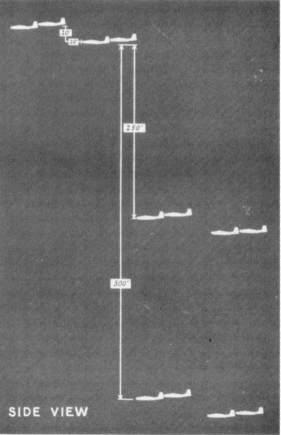

SIDE VIEW

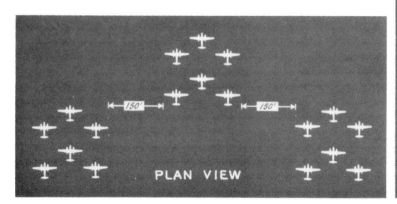

PLAN VIEW

OPENING NAZI "CANS"

Prior to 24 August the only two German destroyers in French waters were the "Elbing" (foreground) and "Seetier" (background) in photo above. Off Le Verdon RAF Beaufighters caught them in rocket and cannon attacks. Returning air crews reported a huge explosion. Next day oil streaks were photographed where strike occurred; neither vessel has since been seen. Below, Beaufighters strafe enemy "M" Class minesweepers in North sea off Holland on 25 August. Twelve airplanes can be counted in the melee. Object that appears to right of photo plane's vertical fin is a barrage balloon.

FACTS ABOUT PLOESTI

Astra Romana, Ploesti's largest refinery, during low-level attack by 8th and 9th AF on 1 August 1943.

DURING the year August 1943-August 1944, Ploesti was subjected to 26 bombing attacks in a campaign to destroy it as Germany's main fuel center. The following 18 pages of IMPACT are devoted to this campaign in the belief that qualified AAF personnel will be interested to examine, through the media presented here, the condition of the first really important strategic target to fall into Allied hands after a long-continued bombardment. It is also felt that a study of the results achieved over this mammoth oil area will be of value to all those concerned with further blows at oil targets, either in Europe or in those areas now owned or held by Japan. No "cost analysis" of the whole campaign has been or should be made here at this time. Nor should final conclusions be drawn regarding the superiority of one kind of attack over another. Ploesti is presented here merely as an historical study of an elaborate tactical problem—solved virtually single-handed by the precision bombardment and tactics of the Fifteenth Air Force.

Continued on next page

WHAT WE DID TO REFINERY PRODUCTION

The importance of Ploesti in the German war economy can hardly be overestimated. It is the largest oil producing area in Axis Europe and contains the largest concentration of refineries. It supplied the Nazis, before it was attacked, with a third of their total liquid fuel requirements, and, more important, with a third of all their gasoline. It is not easy for Americans, who have long lived in an economy of oil abundance, to understand how vital the defense of such a target is to a nation whose oil position is as fundamentally unsound as Germany's. Until Rumania fell into her lap she had been importing crude from this and other European countries to make up the difference between what she produced synthetically at home and what she consumed. Her synthetic production has grown rapidly in the last few years, but (compared with refining crude) the expense and difficulty involved in such production only accentuate how badly she needed a handy natural oil supply of her own.

With this picture of Ploesti clearly in mind, two things about it immediately become apparent: (1) It was certain to be attacked sooner or later. (2) In anticipation of such attacks it was certain to be heavily defended. But, as a corollary to (2), it was probable that the defenses would be rusty if not alerted. Accordingly, when it was decided to attack Ploesti in the summer of 1943, the operation was planned as a one-punch affair designed to achieve maximum effectiveness and surprise at any cost. No preliminary reconnaissance was permitted. The attack was to be made at minimum altitude to insure complete coverage of the target with the relatively small force available. It came off on 1 August 1943. Pictures of it may be seen in IMPACT, Vol. I, No. 6. The elaborate briefing which prepared the way for it is described in IMPACT, Vol. II, No. 2.

At the time of this attack Ploesti was theoretically capable of handling 757,000 metric tons of crude a month, but was actually putting through only 407,000 tons. This was due partly to the fact that Germany was then getting sufficient oil, partly to the fact that the Ploesti fields are gradually drying up, which has had the effect of leaving it with more refinery capacity than crude production. Considering that only 142 tons of bombs were dropped, the damage done on this mission was tremendous. Production for August fell to 269,000 tons. Two of the eleven active refineries in the area were so badly damaged that they were not operated from that time on. Although repairs were pushed rapidly by the Germans, bringing production to 431,000 tons in one month, this should not obscure the real achievement of the low-level attack, which was to destroy almost all the excess refining facilities. From that point on, 400,000 tons a month was virtually a capacity performance.

Then for eight months Ploesti was not disturbed. The Italian campaign, the great air battles in the north to kill off the Luftwaffe, and the endless pre-invasion rail attacks combined during this period to occupy our air forces. However, in April and early May 1944, during blows at the Ploesti rail yards, severe damage was again dealt out to several of the refineries and capacity knocked down to

317,000 tons a month. Careful analysis of these attacks, which proved that oil targets could be hit and knocked out with a reasonable economy of force, was a strong contributing factor in the revision at this time of strategic priorities, placing oil first and putting into action the coordinated campaign against the entire German oil industry.

Now the names of the Ploesti refineries began to become monotonously familiar in 15th Air Force briefings. Four missions were flown against them in May, four in June, five in July and four during the first 19 days of August. By that time production was down 90 percent, and the Russians walked in to take over the remaining 10 percent. At that time only five of the eleven refineries were operating, and one of these, Astra Romana, was supplying over half the output.

Ploesti was never a soft touch. At first it was stubbornly defended by fighters, later by dense smoke and flak installations (see pages 50-53). In five months we lost 223 heavy bombers out of 5,479 effective sorties flown for an over-all combat loss ratio of 3.6 percent. Bombs dropped totaled 13,700 tons, or 2.5 tons per sortie. One hundred and eighty-eight enemy aircraft were destroyed in the area.

These operations, plus the 1943 low-level attack, resulted in a loss to the enemy of 1,334,000 tons of oil, which figures out to 97.5 tons of oil for every ton of bombs dropped. Analysis of the various types of mission flown over Ploesti reveals the following:

	Low-level 1 August 1943	P-38 10 June 1944	High-level 5 April-19 August 1944
Tons of oil production lost	127,000	15,000	1,027,000
Bombers lost	54	24 (P-38s)	223 (also 28 fighters)
Tons of oil destroyed per bomber lost	2,300	625	4,600
Tons of bombs dropped	142	18	13,558
Tons of oil destroyed per ton of bombs dropped	895	830	75.5

From this the August 1943 low-level attack emerges as the most economical by far. It would have been even more so had all elements flown the mission as briefed. However, in behalf of the high-level missions, it should be brought out that these were in a position at the end of their campaign to enormously improve their statistical showing because only by then had they solved the smoke problem, greatest hindrance to the accuracy of their bombing. Finally, in behalf of the P-38 mission, it should be noted that losses were unduly magnified by enemy fighter attacks. If the mission had been conducted two months later, after fighter opposition had been effectively eliminated, and when smoke and flak remained as the hazards, results would have been a great deal better. But it must be remembered that when the mission was flown, the 15th AF was still trying to solve the smoke problem, and could not wait to eliminate fighters.

All production figures in this article, including monthly pre-attack capacities on the map opposite, are from official Rumanian refinery records.

Continued on page 38

Confidential

TO STEAUA
ROMANA 15 MI.
125,000

CONCORDIA VEGA
110,000

XENIA
22,000

ROMANA AMERICANA
92,000

DACIA ROMANA
15,000

PLOESTI

COLOMBIA AQUILA
45,000

STANDARD 36,000
(UNIREA SPERANTZA
33,000 ADD.)

ASTRA ROMANA
146,000
(PHOENIX 65,000 ADD.)

+—+—+ R.R.

——— PRIMARY HIGHWAYS

REFINERY FIGURES SHOW MONTHLY
PRODUCTION IN METRIC TONS

0   1/2   1 MI.

N

CREDITUL MINIER
45,000

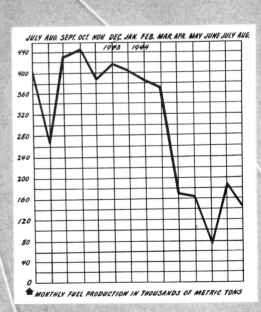

JULY AUG. SEPT. OCT. NOV. DEC. JAN. FEB. MAR. APR. MAY JUNE JULY AUG.
1943   1944

440
400
360
320
280
240
200
160
120
80
40
0

↑ MONTHLY FUEL PRODUCTION IN THOUSANDS OF METRIC TONS

ASTRA ROMANA

Owned by British and Dutch interests, this is the largest and one of the most modern refineries in Rumania. It is equipped with cracking facilities and special wax, polymer and other plants which together handle a fifth of Rumania's total refinery output. It almost completely surrounds a smaller refinery, Phoenix Orion, also British-owned and regarded as a particularly vulnerable target because of the great concentration of its equipment. This includes a lubricating oil plant, one of the few in Rumania. Total capacity of Astra and Phoenix before attacks was 211,000 tons a month. Actual combined production from July 1943 is shown at right. The low-level attack of 1 August 1943 did heavy damage to both, but because of the existence of excess standby facilities, they were soon producing more than before to compensate for reduced capacity at other refineries in the area. The main rail yards at Ploesti lie next to the Astra plant, and when they were attacked in April 1944, the refineries were again damaged. Phoenix was utterly destroyed on 5 May. Production at Astra fell to zero and was expected to remain so for 60 days. Actually recovery was much swifter. This is the only case in the Ploesti campaign where A-2 estimates of production varied more than slightly from the official refinery figures.

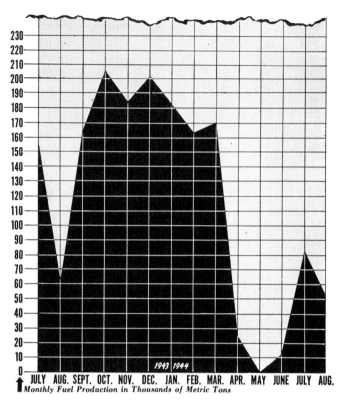

1943 | 1944

JULY AUG. SEPT. OCT. NOV. DEC. JAN. FEB. MAR. APR. MAY JUNE JULY AUG.

Monthly Fuel Production in Thousands of Metric Tons

Low oblique of Astra shows little apparent damage except for smashed tanks. Actually, capacity was down two thirds and due to go lower because of emergency nature of many repairs. Area included in this photo is indicated by dotted line at A in vertical at right, annotations correspond to those on vertical. Large wooden structure at lower left is a cooling tower. New construction (5) is believed to be a catalytic cracking unit, like those in newest U. S. refineries.

Old fashioned pipe still in Trumble Unit (7 in photo below) has been rendered useless by internal blast.

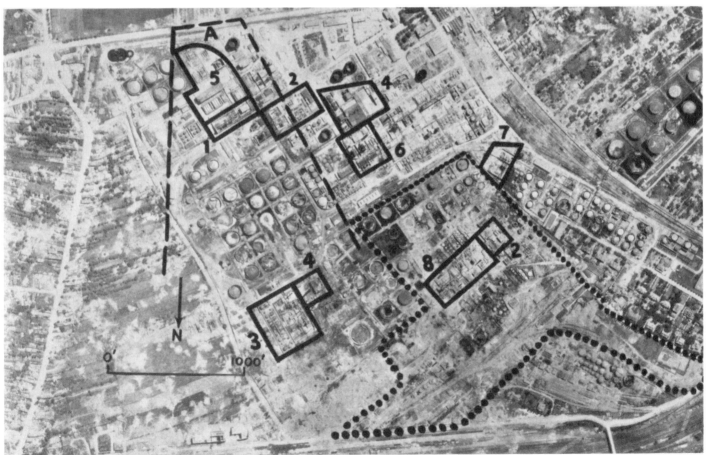

Vertical of Astra Romana and Phoenix Orion (bounded by dotted line) shows effects of numerous attacks. Annotated are stabilization plant (1), doctor plants (2), Dubbs units (3), boiler houses (4), probable catalytic unit (5), McKee unit (6), Trumble unit (7), and pipe stills (8). Most vulnerable part is the boiler house as the steam it produces is used to operate almost all units, is also needed to flush out refinery for speedy shutdown during attacks.

Continued on next page

CREDITUL MINIER

Although this is one of the smaller Ploesti refineries, its equipment is the most up-to-date. It has a sizable Dubbs cracking unit and has the only iso-octane (aviation gasoline) plant in Rumania. Its pre-attack capacity was 45,000 tons a month. Located a few miles south of Ploesti next to a large rail yard, from the air it is one of the most conspicuous refineries in the entire group. The low-level attack of 1 August 1943 did such damage to all its important facilities that production was completely halted and the plant never put back into working order. The Dubbs unit, the power plant and the pipe stills were all wrecked, also a pumping station. The latter is one of several which pump light fuels through pipe lines to the Danube terminal at Giurgiu. The bulk of Ploesti fuels has always been moved by rail.

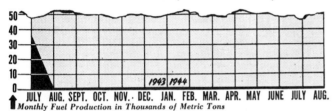

Monthly Fuel Production in Thousands of Metric Tons

Vertical of Creditul Minier shows the following: Pumping station (1), power plant (2), pipe stills (3), Dubbs unit (4), laboratory (5), machine shop (6), treating unit (7). A good deal of this refinery's tankage is still undamaged.

Low oblique of Creditul Minier is annotated to correspond with vertical above. Destruction here and at Colombia Aquila and Steaua Romana testify to soundness of 1943 low-level planning which depended on each plane's hitting the specific building assigned to it. Where formations approached target on proper heading attacks were astonishingly effective. Where they did not, some refineries were missed all together some slightly, some seriously damaged.

STANDARD & UNIREA

Two refineries are contained in the area shown below, Standard Petrol and Unirea Sperantza, with a combined monthly capacity of 69,000 tons. The former had no crude production of its own, and up to the time of the low-level attack was inactive. Undamaged then, it operated at virtual capacity until April 1944, when successive missions seriously damaged it. Unirea was a standby plant for Phoenix Orion. It was put back into production after Phoenix was damaged, then shut down again. Later efforts to get it into production were halted by attacks in the summer of 1944.

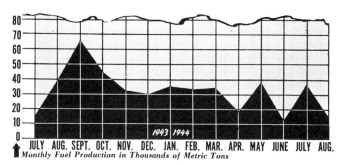

Monthly Fuel Production in Thousands of Metric Tons

Ground photo of Standard plant shows damage to stills in distillation unit. Chimney of boiler house (A in photo below) may be seen in top left. Water tank around chimney does away with need for building separate water tower.

Standard (left) is separated from Unirea (right) as shown by dotted line and by rail yard running through foreground of picture. All Ploesti refineries have extensive rail facilities, relying more on these than on pipe lines for shipment of products. Another line runs along the back of Standard, separating it from the bombed out Concordia munitions works in background of picture (5). Annotated are: Lubricating oil plant (1), distillation plants (2), boiler houses (3).

Continued on next page

ROMANA AMERICANA

Fourth largest in Rumania, this plant escaped damage in August 1943. Thereafter, whenever Ploesti was attacked, citizens fled here for safety in the belief that its ownership by American interests would spare it. Their hopes were shattered in May and June 1944, when Romana fell heir to a series of furious blasts which cut production from 109,000 tons in August 1943 to 12,000 tons in August 1944. Romana was hard to finish off because its vulnerable parts covered a large area, also because it was more heavily protected by blast walls than neighboring refineries. When it was viewed by the entering Russians, its wreckage evoked wondering admiration that the Americans should have dealt so harshly with what was theirs.

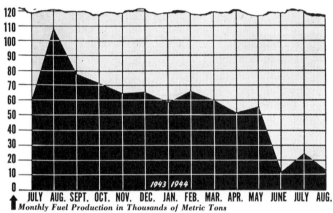

JULY AUG. SEPT. OCT. NOV. DEC. JAN. FEB. MAR. APR. MAY JUNE JULY AUG.
Monthly Fuel Production in Thousands of Metric Tons

First oblique takes in area shown at (A) in vertical at lower left. Tall columns in foreground are cracking towers. They are exceedingly complex in structure. If they can be

Vertical of Romana Americana shows distillation unit (1), boiler houses (2), distillation and cracking (3), machine shop and stores (4). Dotted lines show angles of obliques.

Second oblique takes in area shown at (B) in vertical at left. It shows clearly that the nearest of two boiler houses at (2) has been leveled. The machine shop and storehouses

Confidential

destroyed the usefulness of the refinery is enormously reduced. However, they are ruggedly built, and experience proved that only direct hits could knock them out.

(4) are virtually destroyed. Distillation unit (1) has suffered heavily. Widespread damage to Romana's extensive tankage is plainly visible in this and the photograph above.

Distillation tower for gasoline was knocked over, righted again in an effort to keep refinery running. Note guy wires holding it in place. Small tanks are heat exchangers.

Continued on next page

Confidential

CONCORDIA VEGA

This plant is the third largest in Rumania. It covers 46 acres, with the vital parts confined to 16 acres. Its equipment is modern and includes extensive cracking and distilling facilities. The latter are separated into three independent units, which makes them correspondingly less vulnerable to attack. Concordia's pre-attack capacity was 110,000 tons a month, average production about half of that. Hard hit during the low-level attack, it recovered rapidly, was not hit again until 5 May 1944. It was virtually knocked out on 31 May, but managed to maintain a small output until 10 August when it was finally flattened. Its storage tanks suffered more than any other refinery in Ploesti.

Vertical of Concordia shows distillation plants (1), boiler houses (2), cracking plant (3) before attacks of 1944.

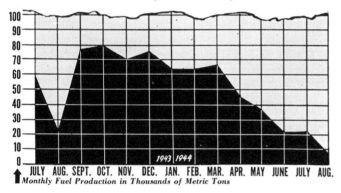

Monthly Fuel Production in Thousands of Metric Tons

JULY AUG. SEPT. OCT. NOV. DEC. JAN. FEB. MAR. APR. MAY JUNE JULY AUG.

1943 1944

Value of blasting tanks like this is that even if distillation facilities are undamaged, production must stop if there is no place to store the gas. Separate distillation units (1) are clearly visible. Closeup opposite was taken at (A).

Closeup of distillation unit shows debris surrounding four damaged fractionating towers, with truncated brick chimney visible just back of them. Dotted lines at (A) in picture on opposite page show the angle at which this photo was taken.

Continued on next page

COLOMBIA AQUILA

About the same size as Creditul Minier, this refinery had a pre-attack capacity of 45,000 tons a month. Its equipment, including a sizable Winkler-Koch cracking plant, was modern. It was virtually erased on 1 August 1943, operations being entirely suspended for 11 months. A trickle of production began to run through it in July and August 1944, as the critical condition of the other refineries in the area began more and more to throw the spotlight on Colombia as the best prospect for repair. Its production record, together with those of Creditul Minier and Steaua Romana, show significant similarities. These three plants were the ones most successfully attacked during the low-level mission and, as was to be expected, were knocked out for a longer period. However, considering the ultimate havoc caused in other refineries, and comparing this with their production records, it appears that Colombia, Creditul and Steaua were out longer in proportion to the damage done than the others. Whether or not this proves anything cannot be stated here now. It may well be that after Romana and Romana Americana were groggy, and in spite of continuing small production, ready to fold up after one more attack or (lacking new equipment) through the mere passage of time.

Vertical of Colombia Aquila is annotated to indicate location of stabilization plant (1), distillation plant (2), boiler house (3). Colombia's vital parts are concentrated in a smaller area than in most of the other Ploesti refineries.

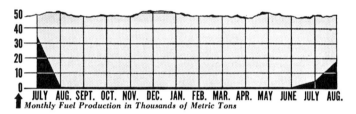

Monthly Fuel Production in Thousands of Metric Tons

Oblique of Colombia Aquila shows many of its tanks intact. Next door is main Girgiu pumping station (4).

XENIA

This is the next to the smallest of the important Ploesti refineries. It covers an area of 39 acres, with the important objectives confined to a little over one acre. Before being attacked, its capacity was 22,000 tons a month. However, it is old-fashioned and poorly equipped compared to the others, and in July 1943 it was not in operation. Ignored during the August 1943 low-level attack, it sprang into production at that time, and was soon operating at capacity in order to handle the continuing flow of crude from the neighboring oil wells, which could not be put through Astra, Phoenix, Concordia, Colombia, Creditul and Steaua because of the damage done to them at that time. Much of Xenia's equipment is obsolete. It has no cracking facilities and its only important installation is a distilling unit. Accordingly, as repairs were pushed at the more efficient refineries, production at Xenia was allowed to fall, reaching zero in March 1944. When attacks were resumed in April and May, Xenia was put into production for the second time. From then on the Germans ran Xenia as hard as they could. It was hit in July, but not seriously damaged. When the Russians arrived it was in operation.

Continued on next page

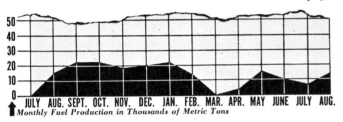

Monthly Fuel Production in Thousands of Metric Tons

Vertical and oblique of Xenia show how this small refinery escaped relatively unscathed. Only important installation is distillation plant and boiler house (1). Some tankage was destroyed. Tank below may be found at (A).

Closeup of tank (A above) that suffered direct hit. Blast wall is typical of those at all Ploesti refineries.

STEAUA ROMANA

Next to Astra, this is the largest refinery in Rumania, with a monthly output of 125,000 tons. It is located 15 miles northwest of Ploesti in the heart of the oil fields. It is well equipped, has extensive cracking facilities and two modern distillation plants, a McKee unit and a Stratford unit. It was here that one of the most heroic actions of the August 1943 low-level attack took place. The formation assigned to it arrived a few minutes after the defenses had been thoroughly alerted by another formation which had swung north after leaving Ploesti. In spite of this, all elements went in exactly as briefed, almost every plane hitting the individual pinpoint assigned to it. This put Steaua flat on its back for four months. It slowly recovered but was hit hard again on 6 May after an attack the night before by the RAF. Output sagged and, according to Rumanian production figures, continued to go down despite a temporary respite from bombing, reaching zero in June. Any further attempts to revive it were canceled out by a final heavy attack on 10 August, the same day that Romana Americana received its coup de grâce.

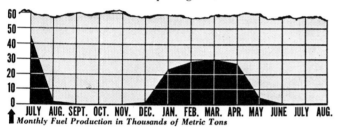

Monthly Fuel Production in Thousands of Metric Tons

Treating plant (above) at Steaua is wrecked. Area in this ground photo is shown at (A) in the vertical at lower left.

Steaua vertical shows process tanks (1), distillation (2, 3), boiler and power houses (4), Dubbs cracking plant (5).

DACIA ROMANA

Last and least of the active Ploesti refineries, Dacia has received less damage than any of them. It is included in this study because it did produce steadily during the period under review and because this puny production became more and more important as the over-all output of the area declined. At the start of the campaign its capacity was only 1.3 per cent of Ploesti's total. By the end of August 1944 this was up to over six percent. Not included in this article are four equally small or smaller refineries, Lumina, Noris, Cometa and Redeventza. These were either so tiny as to be unattractive targets or else were dismantled or hopelessly obsolete. It is believed that some of them were stripped of whatever equipment could be utilized to repair damage in the larger refineries.

Dacia covers an area of 25 acres, with the important objectives confined to three acres. It has a capacity of 15,000 tons a month. Most of its equipment is old and inefficient. It has no cracking facilities, but does contain a distillation unit and a small benzine plant. Almost dormant in July 1943, it was pushed to capacity after the low-level attack, along with Xenia and the other undamaged plants.

Second ground shot (below) at Steaua shows heavy damage to a new installation, possibly a catalytic cracking unit.

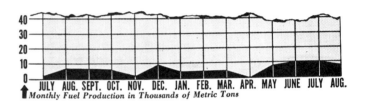

Monthly Fuel Production in Thousands of Metric Tons

Dacia oblique shows boiler house (1), distillation plant (2), benzine plant (3). Five of 2,000 smoke pots are visible.

Continued on next page

Screen is shown developing on 17 August. Romana Americana is at center right. White dots are bomb craters.

SMOKE DEFENSES

The map on the opposite page shows the layout of the smoke defenses of Ploesti as they existed in August 1944. It will be seen that they surrounded the town and all the refineries for a depth of at least a mile. They were stated to be most effective in high humidity, and ineffective in winds exceeding 50 miles an hour. In April the screen was much less elaborate than this, but was enlarged steadily until there were upwards of 2,000 separate installations, the densest concentration in Axis Europe. April and May at-

tacks were not much hampered by smoke, but by June it had become a serious problem. In July five large missions were flown, on only one of which was visual sighting possible, the others being conduced by PFF methods.

Various measures were adopted to deal with this passive but highly effective defense which could completely "black out" the entire area in 20 minutes or less depending on the strength of the wind. The first was a low-level attack on 10 June by 46 bomb-laden P-38s, designed to take the smoke system by surprise. Unfortunately the formation was jumped by defending fighters on the way in, and the element of surprise was lost. However, visibility at the low level was

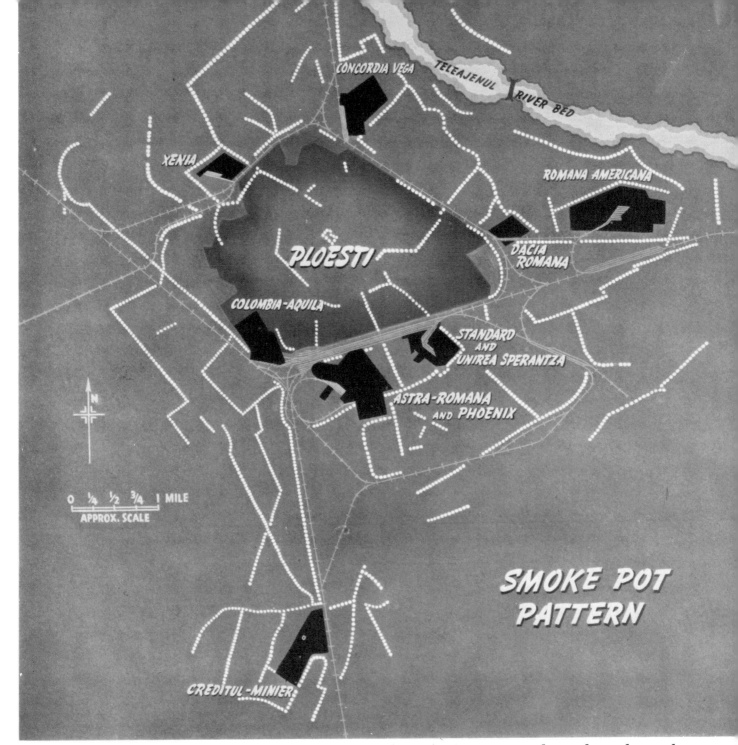

Each dot above is a separate smoke generator consisting (below) of pressure tank, smoke tank, nozzle.

sufficient to permit accurate bombardment. A second experiment involved attempts to circumvent the smoke by "blind bombing." This was done in two ways, by H2X and by offset methods. Both are described in IMPACT, Vol. II, No. 9. A third was tried when it became apparent that surface winds occasionally cleared parts of the target. A P-38 was positioned over Ploesti during the last three attacks in August to broadcast to the approaching bombers which targets were in the clear. Also, during this period an attempt was made to wear out the smoke by attacking over a period of hours. The chief of the Rumanian Passive Defense Command, confirmed the effectiveness of this strategy.

Continued on next page

Giant Wurzburg (left) and Freya (right) were used for early warning and for ground control of enemy fighters.

128 mm railway guns were largest in Ploesti. There were 24 of these, each of which could fire 1 shell every 5 seconds.

Gun laying was handled by small Wurzburgs.

Depth and strength of gun positions is shown here.

FLAK DEFENSES

The flak defenses of Ploesti were among the densest ever flown against by Allied airmen. They protected an area of about 13 miles square with 250 heavy and 400 light guns, not counting numerous Rumanian, Vickers-Armstrong and captured Russian weapons whose effectiveness was questionable. Like the smoke defenses, the Ploesti flak became heavier with the passage of time. Consisting originally of a fairly even scattering of 88 mm batteries throughout the area, they were strengthened with more 88s, with 105s and

with 128 mm railway guns. Our losses to flak rose accordingly, more than doubling in five months.

German radar in Rumania habitually picked up our bombers over Italy and tracked them in to Ploesti with ease, giving an average of 40 minutes in which to close down the refineries, get the civilians under cover and prepare the defenses. This early warning was supplied by giant Freyas. Gun laying was done by small Wurzburgs, one, sometimes two, to a battery. Allied jamming and use of chaff combined to render these useless, forcing the batteries to depend on optical range finding or remote station data. The smoke screen made optical methods useless (in addition to making

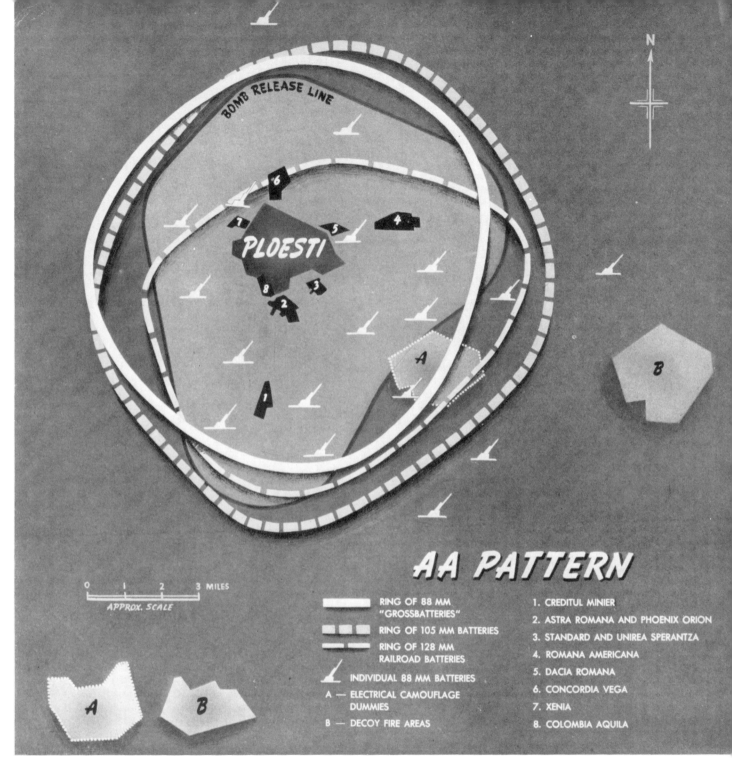

AA PATTERN

APPROX. SCALE
0 1 2 3 MILES

▬▬▬	RING OF 88 MM "GROSSBATTERIES"	
▬ ▬ ▬	RING OF 105 MM BATTERIES	
───	RING OF 128 MM RAILROAD BATTERIES	
⌐	INDIVIDUAL 88 MM BATTERIES	
A —	ELECTRICAL CAMOUFLAGE DUMMIES	
B —	DECOY FIRE AREAS	

1. CREDITUL MINIER
2. ASTRA ROMANA AND PHOENIX ORION
3. STANDARD AND UNIREA SPERANTZA
4. ROMANA AMERICANA
5. DACIA ROMANA
6. CONCORDIA VEGA
7. XENIA
8. COLOMBIA AQUILA

Simplification of AA map shows the relationship of main Ploesti defenses to approximate bomb release line.

the gunners seasick, according to one report) and the Germans eventually resorted to the ringed defense shown on the map above, corresponding roughly to the bomb release line of our bombers. Here they were less bothered by smoke and could concentrate on the "incomers." Most of the 88 mm batteries finally were combined into "grossbatteries," consisting of from 12 to 18 guns each. Predicted fire was almost universally used. Gun positions were well protected by light weapons of 20 and 30 mm (see cut at right). One was occasionally knocked out by a direct bomb hit. Elaborate but ineffective electric camouflage areas and dummy fire installations (see map) also existed at Ploesti.

By radio a P-47 gives lowdown on enemy ground situation to tank columns in Northern France.

THE AIR-TANK TEAM

Tank Leader: "I am receiving fire from enemy tanks in the vicinity of crossroad R-13. Can you get him?"

Pilot: "I'll make a try." *(After flying over the position, he calls back)* "The enemy tank is too close to your position to bomb safely. Back up a short distance, and I'll go after him."

The enemy tank is soon knocked out.

This typical dialogue between a P-47 pilot and a tank leader was overheard on a recent advance in France, such as is illustrated above. It betokens a new kind of air-to-ground cooperation which consists, in brief, of assigning air units—usually P-47s—to cover armored columns.

Here is how it works. High frequency radios are mounted in tanks which move near the head of each column, and are operated by air-ground liaison personnel familiar with their characteristics. Thus, continual radio contact can be maintained between tanks and planes. All communication is by voice, and, to insure recognition, friendly vehicles are marked with red panels.

At a daily conference with the Tactical Air Commands, the G-3 for air requests a certain amount of air cover throughout the day. After the planes are in the air, the armored column control may request the fighters to reconnoiter the roads ahead of the column, or attack specific targets such as enemy tanks or gun positions. One flight generally goes down and works with the column, while another provides high cover. When the lower flight has expended its bombs, it changes position with the high flight. When both are out of ammunition, they may return to base, while a fresh squadron takes their place, thus providing continuous cover for the tanks.

These air-tank teams have met with great success. At first, tanks feared being hit by their own planes, but successful cooperation dispelled this fear. Knowing that "guardian angels" are overhead increases the confidence of tank personnel, and they move boldly ahead.

IMPACT

STRAFING AT HAHA JIMA
See p. 20

DISTRIBUTION:
SQUADRONS

OFFICE OF THE
ASSISTANT CHIEF OF AIR STAFF, INTELLIGENCE
WASHINGTON, D. C.

Vol. 3   No. 1
JANUARY, 1945

IMPACT
Contents
January, 1945

CLASSIFICATION: Overall classification of IMPACT, including text, is CONFIDENTIAL. To insure that this overall classification is recognized, even when pages are torn out for instructional purposes. every single sheet has been stamped CONFIDENTIAL on at least one side. This does not refer to specific photographs whose correct individual classifications are given below:

FRONT COVER THROUGH 4:
  UNCLASSIFIED
5: CONFIDENTIAL
6-7: RESTRICTED
8-9: CONFIDENTIAL
10-13: UNCLASSIFIED
14-15: BOTTOM, CONFIDENTIAL;
  REST UNCLASSIFIED
16: BOTTOM RIGHT, CONFIDENTIAL;
  REST, UNCLASSIFIED
17: CONFIDENTIAL
18-19: BOTTOM LEFT, CONFIDENTIAL;
  REST, UNCLASSIFIED
20-22: UNCLASSIFIED
23: CONFIDENTIAL
24-27: UNCLASSIFIED
28: TOP AND LOWER LEFT, RESTRICTED;
  LOWER RIGHT, CONFIDENTIAL
29: UNCLASSIFIED
30: CONFIDENTIAL
31: CENTER, CONFIDENTIAL; LOWER
  RIGHT, RESTRICTED; REST UN-
  CLASSIFIED
32-33: CONFIDENTIAL
34: UNCLASSIFIED
36-37: CONFIDENTIAL
38-43: UNCLASSIFIED
44-47: CONFIDENTIAL
48-50: UNCLASSIFIED
51 THROUGH INSIDE BACK COVER:
  CONFIDENTIAL
BACK COVER: UNCLASSIFIED

Confidential

TAKEOFF FOR TOKYO, See p. 22

WE ARE FIGHTING ON

Baja railroad bridge across Danube 90 miles south of Budapest looked like this to dicing "Droopsnoot" P-38

Twin Sava river railroad bridges at Belgrade, "White City" of the Partisan Yugoslavs, seen here after 15th AF attacks 3, 6 and 8 Sept. 205 Forts and Libs dropped 565 tons of 1,000-lb. RDX bombs at cost of one B-24 due to IAH flak.

Red Army is Beneficiary of MAAF

Their efforts somewhat obscured by the magnitude of events elsewhere, fliers of MAAF have been contributing substantially to the campaign against the Hun on the Eastern front.

Outstanding example of this is the "Balkan Strangle" conducted last fall when the Russian armies began advancing into Hungary, Czechoslovakia and Yugoslavia. The campaign was similar to the earlier "strangle" operation in Italy (IMPACT, Vol. 2, No. 7). In one month during the Balkan campaign, 15th AF and RAF components of the Strategic Air Forces flew 53 missions and dropped 8,000 tons of bombs on rail and road bridges, marshaling yards and ferry installations. The high-altitude attacks on bridges were particularly effective and for a long period, through rail traffic became almost impossible for the enemy.

THE EASTERN FRONT, TOO

after strike by 15th AF B-24s 21 Sept. MAAF played big role in strangling German escape routes from Balkans.

"Strangle" Operation in Balkans

As soon as Rumania capitulated and the Russians broke through to Turnu-Severin (The Iron Gate) on the Danube in August, the "strangle" started in earnest. "Rat Week" at the beginning of September saw the 15th AF operate directly with Russian and Partisan ground forces. The 15th's contribution was an outstanding record of bridge-busting. Eight bridges in Hungary and Yugoslavia, four of them across the Danube, were rendered impassable between 2 and 25 September; several were completely destroyed, as shown on these pages. Reconnaissance disclosed that during "Rat Week" heavies cut all main rail lines from Bulgaria and Yugoslavia to Budapest and Vienna. December saw the 15th AF cut loose farther west, against communications in Austria and Southern Germany.

Attempts of Germans to cross Morava river at Kraljevo, Yugoslavia, proved futile when 48 15th AF B-24s on 19 Sept. snapped temporary wooden structure above, next to wrecked rail bridge, with 500-lb. RDX bombs from 18,000 ft.

Continued on next page

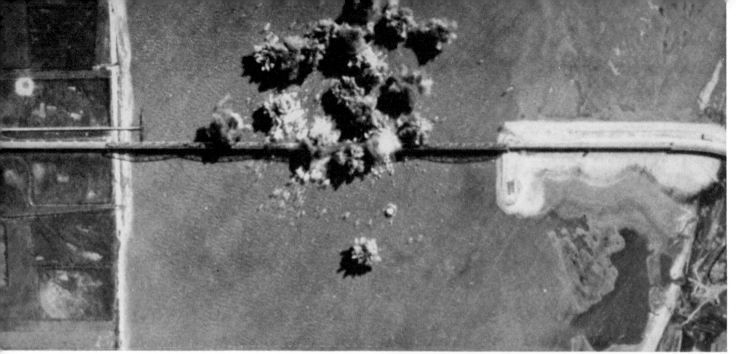

Proof of the Believing is in Seeing

The Russians refused to believe that high-altitude bombing could be accurate enough to knock out a bridge until they saw these photographs of what 15th AF heavies did to the great Pancevo bridge across the Danube at Belgrade, Yugoslavia.

Pancevo is only one of a series of bridges attacked during "Rat Week," September climax to the Balkan "Operation Strangle" described on the previous page. Seldom has there been a more graphic example of accurate precision bombing.

Top above: Thousand-lb. GP bombs make perfect pattern on Pancevo bridge from 24,000 ft. Strike on 3 September was carried out by 54 15th AF B-17s with 25 P-38 escorts. **At right and below:** second span from south end of bridge is completely gone. Heavy damage was also done to piers at north end.

AAF's jet bomb, JB-2, flares away some energy in Wright Field wind tunnel during recent ATSC experiments.

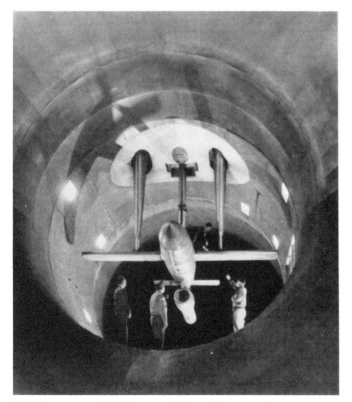

"Chinese copy" of German's V-1, JB-2 is studied from all angles, had to be fixed bottoms up in wind tunnel tests.

U. S. BUZZ BOMB

The picture above, which starts our story with a flash and a hiss, gets you about as close to a buzz bomb as you'd want to get. This version of the German V-1 was made by ATSC, and the photo was shot late on a Sunday night, when Wright Field's wind tunnel could operate without sucking too much power out of nearby Dayton's lighting system.

Cameramen from Tech Data Lab took this picture through a thick glass window. The JB-2 was actually upside down in the tunnel, but the photo above has been inverted to show you what the pilots saw who were up among these things, shooting them down, when the robots were swarming across the channel skies towards England.

The upper cylinder seen here with its tail aflame is the JB-2's propulsion unit, 11 ft. 3 in. long. Diameter is 1 ft. 10¾ in. at the forward end, 1 ft. 4 in., for the rear half. The unit is of the simple impulse duct type, with 40-50 impulses per second. It burns a low-grade aviation fuel.

The JB-2 carries one 2,000-lb. warhead. The AAF is also experimenting with other jet-driven missiles, one of which is expected to contain 4,000 lbs. of explosive, but the present story is concerned only with the JB-2. The next two pages will show you pictures of its mechanism and launching devices, and the bomb in action at Eglin Field Proving Ground.

Continued on next page

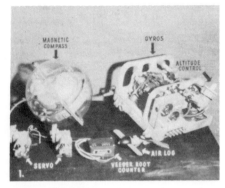

Some innards of JB-2, and how they are installed. Photo No. 1 shows important parts of control devices; No. 2 shows some of them in place. In No. 3, compass is being "swung."

Germans adjust compasses in non-magnetic buildings; at Eglin Field Proving Ground, this is done in wooded place away from launching track and other magnetizing influences.

What Makes Buzz Bombs Tick

Some idea of the complications involved in putting together and launching the JB-2 may be gained from what is pictured on these two pages.

The servos and the gyro unit seen in Photo No. 1, above, perform the task of moving the jet bomb's controls. They are monitored by the magnetic compass installed in the nose. The little propeller-like device known as the air log is fitted onto the front of the nose, where it spins during the flight. It clicks at every fifteenth turn, and this action is registered on the counter, which measures the amount of air passed through and is pre-calculated for range. When the target is reached, this counter starts the mechanism which fires two electric detonators in the tail, and these position the elevators for the dive.

The JB-2's launching track is 500 ft. long with an incline of six degrees. When the bomb is ready on the cart, the jet system is turned on: air flow is started by a compressor connected with the engine, fuel is forced in, and spark plug ignited. The engine carries on without further help from the ignition system or the compressor air flow. Engine runs at comparatively low efficiency until high speeds are reached.

After the jet system is started, the five rockets at the rear of the cart are set off—then cart and bomb go whizzing up the track.

The stubbornest problem in connection with takeoffs is that of speed. With a 155-ft. ramp, the Germans got about 250 mph in one second. Present AAF scheme gets this speed in about 2 seconds, using 400 feet. This has important advantages, now secret.

Cart for JB-2 shows where bomb is placed for launching. The five covered cylinders at the rear are rockets which will give the cart its initial velocity.

Bomb on track, with electric cables running back to control structure, the squat, fortress-like building of very heavy concrete seen beyond the launching tracks.

Confidential

JB-2 waits on track, which has small stakes at left containing devices for helping to measure takeoff speed.

Zoom-zoom-zoom, and the JB-2 begins its Wellsian flight into space. At one Eglin Field Proving Ground test, jet bomb reached 6,000 ft. altitude, was then shot down by ob-serving plane. In the flight pictured above, the rocket-thrust was unusual in that it propelled cart beyond the ramp. The robot levelled off at 3,500 ft. before it flew out of sight.

Airplane pick-up test ready to start at Muroc Lake, Calif., with P-47's tow-bridle loop strung to poles.

B-17 PICKS UP P-47 AT 160 MPH IN RESCUE TESTS

Propeller rigged for pick-up, P-47 waits with pilot in cockpit. Experiment has been successfully conducted with and without props. When used, prop is lashed tight as above.

Electric winch in this C-47 resembles larger installation in B-17s. Winch and twin pulleys reel out tow rope as necessary to decrease pressure and "g" force on the towed airplane.

To solve the problem of AAF fighters downed in inaccessible combat areas, the Equipment Laboratory of the ATSC at Wright Field has been experimenting with plane-snatching methods. The photos on these two pages show how a B-17 can scoop up a P-47 and tow it to a repair base.

The technique and equipment for this project are similar to those used in the human pick-up (see IMPACT, Vol. 2, No. 11) and in the old glider tow-off. Experiments have also been made with P-51s, which have been lifted from the ground by B-17s, C-47s, and B-25s. The medium bombers have worked best with Mustangs, just as the heavy bombers have proved most effective with Thunderbolts. Pilots, particularly those in the fighter planes, must be highly skilled, and they require special training for this type of work.

The aircraft that is to be raised has the pick-up loop of its tow bridle strung across the tops of two upright poles, as shown in the picture above. The rescuing plane swoops low, dragging a hook at the end of the wooden arm shown in the middle photo on the opposite page. The P-47s in these experiments have had their takeoff distance reduced to the astonishingly small space of 500 ft. When the planes arrive at the designated bases, the towed aircraft release themselves, and their pilots make dead stick landings. Fighters with props release by electrically-controlled T-D explosive connector links (cylinder in front of spinner, photo in middle, left). If prop is off, standard glider release is used.

Pictures at right show Sinbad trick operating, with B-17 flying low at 160 mph for contact, then hoisting P-47 upward. Poles that hold tow-rope loop are not seen; they are out of sight to left in first two photos, to right in next two. Bottom picture, with photo plane's wing cutting across left edge, shows prop-less P-47 being pulled along in level flight.

At start of 1943, AAF from New Guinea, Tarawa, and China hammers only at periphery of huge Jap Empire.

AAF IN THE PACIFIC: 1944 REVIEW

Presented as a quick, year's end review, these three maps show the progress made by the AAF in the Pacific during the past year. Individual campaigns are not delineated. Solid red arrows show roughly where separate Army Air Forces operated, but make no attempt to trace their courses. The two big, light red arrows show the general direction of the main drives: Nimitz from the East and MacArthur from the south. Areas of principal Naval action are symbolized by battleships. Jap-held territory is shown in black.

Situation at end of 1943. Based firmly on Guadalcanal, northeast New Guinea, Tarawa and Makin, the AAF strikes at Rabaul, Wewak, Kwajalein, and other Jap strongholds in the Marshalls. The 10th and 14th AF lash out in Burma and China, harassing Jap shipping, cooperating with Allied land armies. But as yet the double drive toward Japan's Inner Empire is in its infancy.

Situation on 1 September, 1944. Great progress has been made in eight months. The pattern for triphibious war, involving AAF and carrier-based planes, land and Naval action, is clearly established. Result: we have won bases on Kwajalein, the Admiralties, and other strategic spots. Japs are left to rot in Rabaul and mould in the Marshalls. Truk, too, is being emasculated, and from its new Saipan base, "The Leaping 7th" is attacking the Bonins. Possibly most important, B-29s have already begun their giant strides toward Japan, striking at steel targets in Anshan and Yawata. MacArthur's drive has virtually ousted the enemy from New Guinea, and new AAF bases bring our bombers within easier range of Japan's rich resources in the East Indies. A milestone is reached on 1 September when B-24s hit the Philippines (Davao) for the first time since 1942.

Situation at end of 1944. Converging in a terrific explosion of synchronized air, land, and sea power, the twin drives of Nimitz and MacArthur now point at the heart of Japan's Inner Empire. In the short period of four months, our forces have set up bases on Guam, Palau, and the Philippines. Now for the first time our Air Forces, hitting from East and West, are engaged in the same combined operations, with B-29s packing a major wallop. This teamwork was exemplified by the October attacks on Formosa, when B-29s, striking from China in coordination with carrier-based planes, knocked out the Okayama aircraft plant. This bore an obvious relationship to the historic Leyte landings, as it cancelled out aircraft that might have reinforced the Japs in the Philippines. On 24 November the first Saipan-based B-29s hit Tokyo. From almost every point of the compass, seven U. S. air forces, including the XX and XXI Bomber Commands, now keep the Japs dizzy wondering where the next bombs will fall. On the next 23 pages, you will see how and where some of these Pacific air forces operate.

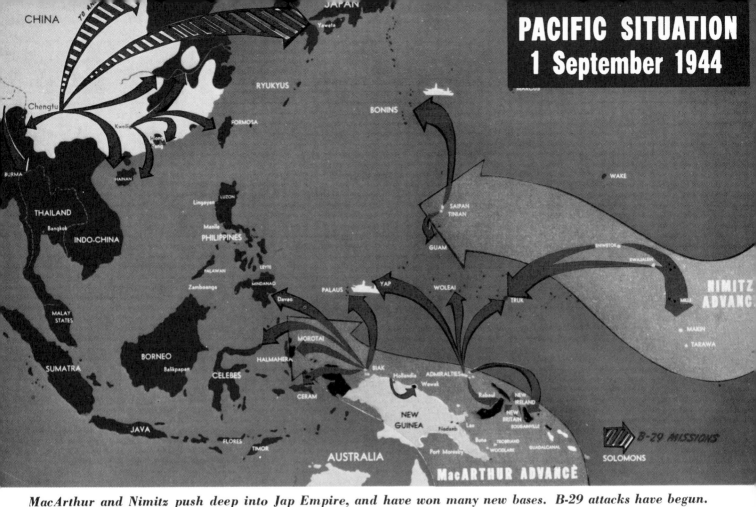

MacArthur and Nimitz push deep into Jap Empire, and have won many new bases. B-29 attacks have begun.

War against Japan reaches new intensity; great galaxy of air, land, sea forces engage in combined attacks.

Leyte-bound Jap task force cork-screws in vain to avoid bombs of 13th AF Libs on 26 Oct. west of Panay, P. I.

FEAF Works Out on Jap Fleet, Sinks Pair of Light Cruisers

The Damon and Pythias act of AAF and Navy in the Pacific again came into the spotlight during the great October victory over the Japanese fleet in Philippine waters.

Landings at Leyte faced the enemy with a critical decision. At all costs they had to prevent the first step in the retaking of the islands, because loss of the Philippines would mean an end to control of the South China Sea and of all lanes to the South. This would eventually place Malaya and the NEI in much the same position as New Guinea and New Britain—mere limbs for us to prune sooner or later. With this ominous prospect beginning to materialize at Leyte, the Japs at long last sent out their will-o-the-wisp navy in force. Three elements of this fleet were routed by the U. S. Navy east and south of Luzon and Leyte.

A fourth major task force of 12 vessels seen above was headed for Leyte undetected until it was successfully attacked on the morning of 26 October in the Sulu sea by the self-styled "Long Rangers" (B-24s) of the FEAF. Other units fleeing from the Suriago strait naval engagement were caught by the FEAF southwest of Negros.

Photos at right show a Kuma class cruiser taking evasive action while being attacked by the "Bomber Barons" of the 13th AF off Negros. The B-24s used 1,000-lb. and 500-lb. GP bombs from 9,700 feet. Four direct hits caused fires and explosions amidships; the cruiser sank three hours later. Nearby the same morning 5th AF Libs made it two Kuma class cruisers for the day when they hit another which blew up and sank when the magazine exploded.

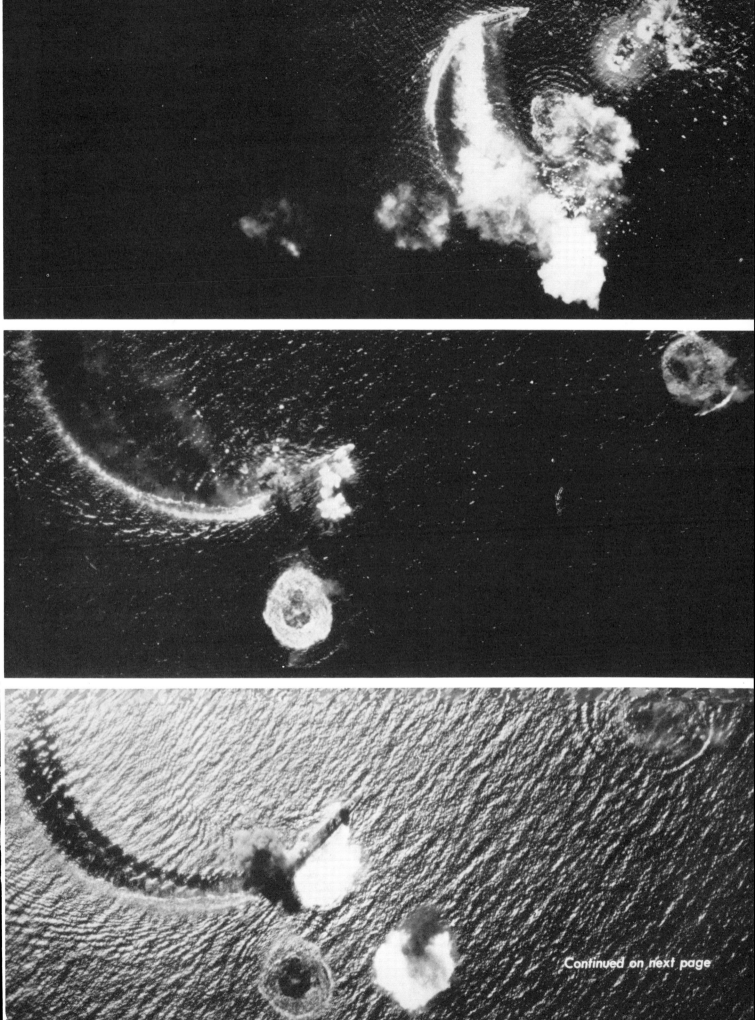

Continued on next page

13th AF "Long Rangers"

FEAF "Long Rangers" in their 26 October strike (shown here) on Jap battlewagons in the Sulu sea, successfully solved the problem of hitting moving naval targets from high level. The lead bombardier of the formation explains his solution as follows:

"By describing a course at right angles to the enemy fleet while we sought a suitable target, we caused most of the AA fire to be aimed on an arc and gave Jap gunners problems of deflection firing. Formation lost 500 feet on approach run; as a result the first AA fire was 500-800 feet above.

First verticals (both photos above) of Yamato class battleship—largest in the Jap navy—show the huge ship taking evasive action during attacks by "Long Rangers" of 13th AF on 26 Oct. Two direct hits, many near misses were scored.

Panorama of Jap fleet units in hiding at Brunei bay, NEI, on 7 Nov. following defeat at Leyte shows (1) BBs,

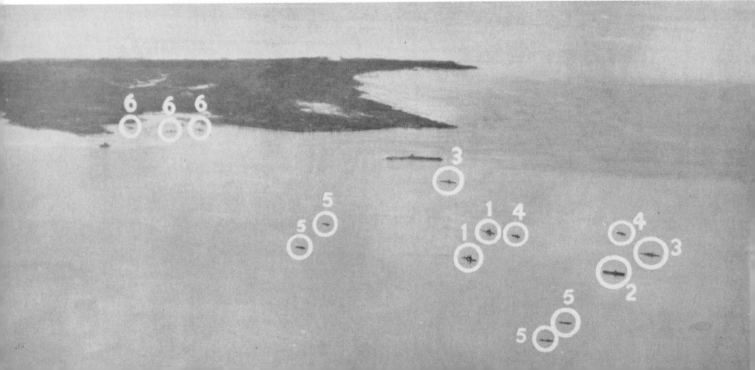

Ride Against Nip BBs

"All the warships took evasive action with a left turn. Flak threw my bombsight off level twice during the run, but course was not difficult to hold. A few seconds before bomb release point the Kongo type BB's bow wave began to shift. As the BB committed itself to a right turn, 4° drift correction before "bombs away" helped solve the course problem. Because the bombsight cannot solve curved course problems, the impact point had to be estimated. The BB had only 28.75 seconds for evasion from bombing altitude of 9,000 feet."

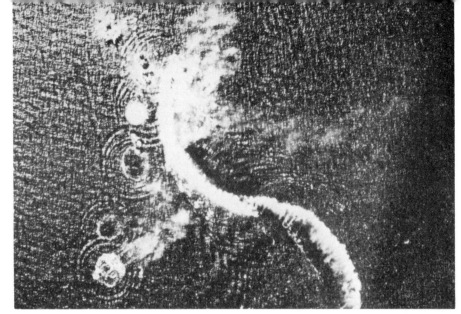

Kongo class battleship (top) is bracketed by 1,000-lb. bombs during 26 Oct. strike on Jap task force off Panay.

Lower photo was taken after Libs made two direct hits from 9,000 ft. All 27 planes were holed by accurate heavy flak.

(2) CV, (3) CAs, (4) CLs, (5) DDs, and (6) MVs. FEAF on 16 Nov. made 5 hits here on a BB, 4 on a CA.

Continued on next page

Explosions among grounded aircraft and cratered runways were results of 6 Nov. FEAF strike at Lahug, Cebu.

Airfields Hit Too

Part of FEAF's and of every air force's job in the Pacific is the monotonous task of neutralizing Jap airfields. It is a steady process of attrition, of bombing fields, shops, hangars and other facilities and continuing to hit them so repairs cannot be completed. Shown here are three typically successful FEAF airfield strikes that helped reduce Jap air attacks on General Mac-Arthur's troops following the Leyte landings.

At right is oblique of Puerto Princesa airdrome, Palawan, showing 1,000-lb. bombs walking neatly down runway during 28 Oct. attack by FEAF. Among 23 destroyed and 10-15 damaged are (1) Bettys and (2) unidentified S/E aircraft. Libs unloaded 72 tons from low altitude, did not meet AA or E/A.

13th AF "Long Rangers" hit jack-pot again with 65 tons of 500-pounders on Dumaguete airfield, Negros, 11 Nov.

VOLCANIC BONINS RE-ERUPT UNDER 7th & 20th AF BOMBS

Our advances in the Pacific are giving old-time 7th AF pilots new lessons in geography. In contrast to the lush tropical atolls of the south and central Pacific, they are now pounding rugged, dismal targets such as the vital Volcano and Bonin islands shown on the next four pages.

Objectives of recent 7th and 20th AF neutralization attacks, these islands are part of a chain known as the Nanpo Shoto. Extending 700 nautical miles in a north-south line from the entrance to Tokyo Bay to within 300 miles of the northern Marianas, the Nanpo Shoto form part of the inner ring of the Jap empire defenses. Strength is concentrated in the more southerly part, where there are airfields on heavily defended Iwo Jima (Sulphur island) of the Volcanos and on Chichi Jima (Baily island) of the Bonins, a potent seaplane and naval base.

The Bonins are strategically important because they lie directly on our Superfortress' route to Tokyo. Therefore, it is imperative that they be kept neutralized. Also the Japs are using Iwo and Chichi as bases for effective attacks on our B-29s in the Marianas (see page 32).

The islands in this group are extinct volcanos. Their shores are mostly steep rocky cliffs with few narrow sandy beaches in small coves. On Iwo, nauseous sulphur gases constantly bubble from countless blowholes. Iwo's small plateau has two air strips and a third under construction.

Continued on next page

In Parking Areas on Isley Field, Saipan, these 7th AF Libs await orders to attack the Bonins and Volcanos.

CHICHI JIMA

FUTAMI KO
HARBOR

Bleak volcanic peaks mark formidable Chichi Jima, the most heavily defended island of the Bonins. Shipping at

Crippled Futami Ko harbor, Chichi Jima, during 7th AF attack 19 Nov. Considerable previous damage to naval base

FUTAMI KO HARBOR

NEW TYPE LST

BOW
LARGE MV
STERN

SMALL MVs

LST

HOKKO MARU

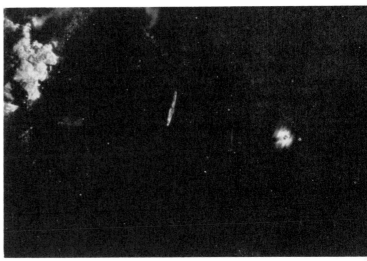

New-type Jap auxiliary transport similar to our LST rides at anchor in Futami Ko harbor, Chichi Jima, just as first bomb falls nearby during 19 Nov. 7th AF shipping strike.

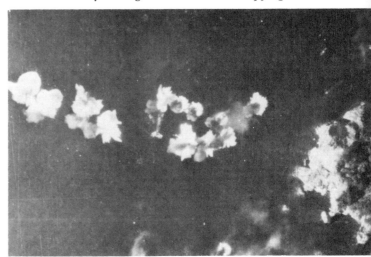

Taken a few seconds after the picture above, this view from 15,000 ft. shows sticks from the Liberators straddling the transport. One hit from a 500-pounder did the trick neatly.

Naval base at Futami Ko is deluged by 7th AF bombs on 2 Nov. On this same mission 21 B-24s with 30 tons sank one AK (cargo ship), set another afire, damaged two others.

Continued on next page

Chichi was target for 15 7th AF B-24s on 19 November.

(lower right) and chief city Omura (top right) is evident.

TROYED HANGARS

EAPLANE BASE

OMURA

NAVAL INSTALLATIONS
DESTROYED

Haha Jima Retto (above), southernmost of the Bonins, has no airfield, but an excellent anchorage for shipping. Despite accurate flak, B-24s on 16 Nov. here scored one hit on Jap sub chaser from 17,000 feet, two near misses on another.

Terraced hillsides at Higashi Minato bay (below), overlooking ruined Kitamura town on northwest coast of Haha Jima, are cleared for growing sugar cane and fruits. Vegetation in Bonins forms dense tangle of tropical undergrowth.

Small Jap craft hug steep cliffs of Haha Jima in attempt to avoid strafing of low-flying 7th AF Libs on 19 Nov. (see

Jap phosphorous bombs (above right) failed to halt 7th AF attack on Iwo Jima airfield installations 4 Nov. One TE and one SE aircraft were destroyed on ground. Five unaggressive fighters were airborne; intense AA damaged 5 B-24s.

Frags sprinkle Iwo Jima like summer shower on 4 Nov. Biggest mission to date on Iwo was 6 Dec. when 82 B-29s of 20th AF and 102 7th AF Libs bombed by PPI without loss through 10/10ths cloud. Results were unobserved.

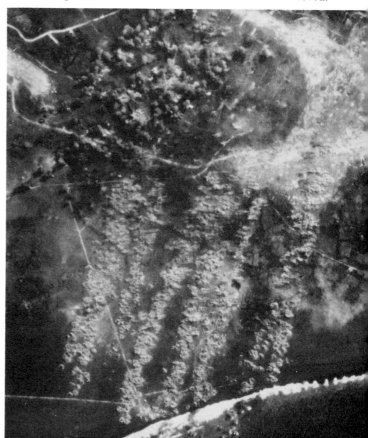

front cover). Pilots often must fly low in Bonins, because thick cumulus cloud cover exists some 50 percent of time.

SAIPAN: B-29 SPRINGBOARD TO TOKYO

One truck every 40 seconds moves out of enormous Saipan quarry, carrying coral to surface strip.

Building the Base

Washington engineers said it couldn't be done. Tokyo Rose over the Japanese radio said it couldn't be done. But the Aviation Engineers did it. They overcame all the technical problems of building giant, B-29 runways on Saipan. Today this fifteen-mile-long island in the Marianas, in addition to being a base for B-24s attacking the Bonins (see page 17), has become a springboard to Tokyo. Here, and on the next 11 pages, are pictures showing how the base

was built and used for the first historic land-based bombing mission over the Jap capital.

Six days after we took Saipan on 14 June, Aviation Engineers calling themselves "Flying Castles," came ashore and began the big job. Within 24 hours they had filled in some 600 craters made by our air and naval bombardment. Then they added 1,000 feet to Aslito strip, now part of Isley field, and started to build the new heavy bomber strip.

To get tons of coral, needed for construction, an army of bulldozers went to work and literally chewed down two coral mountains. One is shown above. A procession of more than

Confidential

From Longest Runway in the Pacific, B-29s on 24 Nov. 1944 Roared Away to Nippon, opening a new phase of the campaign to wreck Jap war industry

Asphalt topping is half done on "Isley No. 1," longest strip in the Pacific. It is 8,500 feet by 200 feet.

100 four-ton trucks carried away coral shavings to provide surfacing for runways, hardstands, roads.

Another necessity was liquid asphalt to be used as a final surfacing. This problem was what made the Washington experts warn that "black top couldn't be used in the Marianas," because liquid asphalt cannot be shipped. But it was decided to ship hard asphalt in drums. An ingenious "homemade" melting plant was rigged up by the engineers out of a former Jap sugar boiler, with a smokestack made of welded oil drums. Seven hundred tons of liquid asphalt were produced on Saipan daily.

Getting the runways built was considered such a priority job that not even the General's jeep was allowed to travel around the island without carrying coral. Normally the engineers would have built living quarters first, but not this time. Officers and men dug in to erect their own tents, mess halls, offices, showers and latrines. Building the field and the complex system of hardstands went on all night under batteries of spotlights. One observer said it looked as if Henry Kaiser had taken over the island. How Saipan received its first "Super" visitors, and how they prepared and took off for their first "Super" mission is depicted on next pages.

Continued on next page

Making familiarization flights over the Marianas soon after their arrival, B-29s flew same formations they

No redcaps unloaded luggage for crews of newly arrived B-29, but they got the job done easily by tossing their luggage from plane to truck, parked in foreground.

"Here's where you live." Trucks move luggage to huts where crews live in relative

29s Arrive and Settle Down

While the Saipan base was being readied for its new tenants, the tenants themselves were on their way. By 6 November a considerable number of B-29s had finished the first leg of their journey from the U. S. to John Rodgers airport near Honolulu, and were all set to take off again. Their only stop between Oahu and Saipan was Kwajalein.

Soaring high over the Pacific, this was the last, long peaceful journey these planes would enjoy until some would fly back again to the States. The crew took turns sleeping on the two berths in each Superfort. At Saipan they had a big reunion with ground crews who had made the trip by water. On these two pages you see how their new island home looked to them immediately upon arriving.

adopted later on Tokyo missions.

One small jeep, like friendly pup, greets and leads newcomer to hardstand.

comfort except when Jap night raiders force them to jump for their foxholes.

Journey's end—for awhile. B-29 parks in the tent area of the 804th Engineer Aviation Battalion which went into Saipan immediately after the assault forces.

Continued on next page

Work and Play

Mopping-up operations by crew of the "Special Delivery" make the plane look spruce after trip.

At lunch hour a mechanic catches up on sleep lost during Jap air raids.

Not in a bathtub, mechanic inspects cowling as part of 50-hour inspection.

"Damit," pet pup, gets snapped in rear escape hatch with Sgt. L. L. Lee.

Not strictly in the line of duty, but very beneficial to morale is this lesson on the fine points of a B-29's top forward turret. The teacher is Corporal Ralph Taylor, a tail-gunner from Langford, South Carolina, and his pretty blond pupil is Lieutenant Helda Halverson of Chicago, one of the flight nurses now on duty with the XXI B.C. on Saipan.

Tokyo Rose

"Tokyo Rose" returns safely to Saipan on 12 November after getting much-needed recon photos of Tokyo.

Musashino aircraft factory, the future B-29 target at Tokyo, was covered by "Tokyo Rose" in the first U. S. mission over the Japanese capital since Lt. General Doolittle's famous visit in April, 1942.

Captain R. S. Steakley poses beside his plane after winning Distinguished Flying Cross for leadership during the first B-29 recon. flight over Tokyo.

Continued on next page

Ready, Set, Go

Piled three-high, these 500-lb. GP babies wait to be dropped on Tokyo's doorstep by Super-storks.

A 500-lb. aimable cluster is hauled to a B-29. Of the total bomb load on first Tokyo mission on 24 November, about two thirds were 500-lb GP bombs, one third was incendiaries.

Fusing Bombs is supervised by Ordnance officer. Bombs shown here are incendiaries. Tokyo was blasted later by an all-incendiary mission flown by B-29s.

Confidential

.50 cal. ammunition in quantities is loaded aboard a B-29 in preparation for the first bombardment mission.

"Shady Lady" gets her upper forward turret adjusted by an armament man before she pays a call on Tokyo.

Fueling the B-29s from fuel trucks is one more crucial operation leading up to the historic first take off.

Navigator, Lt. Irving Blumefield, checks his equipment—one of last minute jobs that make for success.

Brig. General Emmett O'Donnell, who will lead the mission, briefs his officers with maps of the Tokyo area.

Last check is made by Brig. General O'Donnell and his pilot, Maj. Brogan, just as they prepare to take off.

They're off. Crowds of engineers and ground crewmen watch the giant planes begin first Tokyo mission.

Continued on next page

Bombs Fall on Tokyo

Bombs over Tokyo on 24 November plunge towards the primary target (bottom, center), the important Musashino aircraft engine plant. Due to bad weather, which changed during the mission from 2/10 to 9/10 undercast, this is best of the photos showing the attack. Heavy clouds during later missions continued to make picture coverage a problem.

Confidential

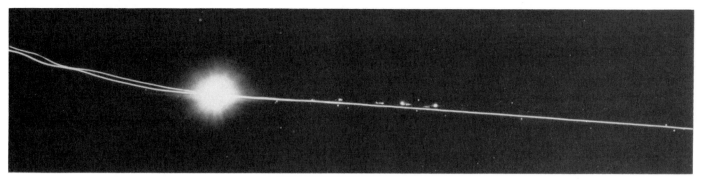

This streak of light meant success. It is the pattern made by the landing lights of a homecoming B-29.

Left-overs! This vertical picture taken from the inside of a B-29 shows a gunner sorting ammunition left over after the first mission. But the Japs will get it sooner or later.

Boxscore & Battle Damage

When more than 100 B-29s lined up at dawn on 24 November, they began not only the first Saipan-based attack on Tokyo. They started a new phase of the Jap air war. What added most to their achievement is the fact that it was followed up again and again, with more and more success.

Hitting in two waves, totalling 35 planes, the Superforts began to dump their bombs on the primary target about noon (see p. 30) from 27,000 to 33,000 feet. An added 54 planes hit industrial targets along Tokyo's waterfront. About 125 Jap aircraft provided the fighter opposition, which, for the most part, was "moderate." The greatest percent of attacks came from level and high front. Flak was heavy, but damaged only one of our aircraft. One B-29 was lost after colliding with a fighter, and another was forced to ditch. Its crew was saved. Our claims: seven destroyed, 16 probables, five damaged.

By 18 December the XXI Bomber Command had hit Tokyo three more times, Iwo Jima once, and had made two successful attacks on the Mitsubishi aircraft plant at Nagoya. The Saipan-Japan express was really rolling at last.

Close but not too close came the 20mm. Jap shell over Tokyo that ripped the hole in this B-29's de-icer boot. It is inspected here by Sergeant Sam Bolinsky, left gunner.

Tony collided with this No. 3 engine of a B-29 on a 3 December Tokyo mission. Plane got back to base, but Tony lost control, collided with another Tony. Both went down.

Continued on next page

The Japs Hit Back

Anybody who expected that the Japs would hit Saipan in retaliation for our attacks on Tokyo was not disappointed. Between 1210 and 1455 on 27 November (Saipan time) 16 Zeke fighters made a determined assault upon the B-29 parking area at Isley Field. Attacking at minimum altitude, the Zekes destroyed three B-29s, as shown in these pictures, and damaged others.

The effect of Jap raids on Saipan is described informally but well in a letter from an officer on Saipan dated 7 December. "There are Jap raids galore. Those babies aren't fooling. Ever since the first Tokyo raid they have come over night after night and despite the great numbers of planes we shoot down, they manage to get in their damage and keep everyone on the alert. It's getting so everyone scrams at the slightest noise and we really have built some sturdy foxholes."

Zeke's tail (left) ends up by tail of B-29 which it rammed and destroyed. After Jap attack four charred motors of a B-29 tell one side of the story.

Bulldozer fights fire among smoking Here is the other: Of the 16 attacking

wreckage of B-29s. B-29 wing is covered with foamite, a snowy-looking chemical used to extinguish flames. Japanese planes, 13 were destroyed—six by fighters, seven by AA. The other three are listed as possibles.

B-25s AT HONG KONG
Low-Level Attack Sinks 5 Ships

This photo sequence of B-25s over Hong Kong harbor on 16 October shows part of the attack in which eight low-sweeping Mitchells of the 11th and 491st squadrons, 341st Bomb Group (M), using 500-lb. GP bombs, sank two 6,000-ton freighters, two 6,000-ton tankers, one 4,000-ton freighter, and damaged one 6,000-ton transport and four other ships. The B-25s released at 75-100 foot altitudes.

The attack was accompanied by a high-level B-24 assault on the Kowloon docks (see IMPACT, Vol. 2, No. 12). The heavies and mediums were escorted by P-51s and P-40s. Of eight attacking Nip fighters, one was destroyed. Two B-25s were damaged severely, but all returned.

1 **B-25** on low-level run at Hong Kong has just scored a direct hit on one ship in background and is starting to swerve to right toward another victim.

2 **String of** bombs is dropped on second target with many obvious "overs." Note center ship was not attacked.

3 **Geysering bomb** bursts show target No. 2 was lucky although near miss behind stern may have caused damage.

A Great Air Force is Great No Longer. Reasons: Allied Growth, Allied Attacks and Its Own Mistakes

When the German Army rolled into Poland in 1939, it was backed up by the finest air force in the world. It was twice the size of the Royal Air Force, three times the size of the U. S. Army Air Corps. It was a formidable weapon of both long-range and high-performance fighters, bombers of all kinds, troop carrier, transport, long and short range reconnaissance and other types. Although regarded by German military minds as primarily a ground support weapon, they believed it to be equipped for any kind of aerial warfare. Its planes were uniformly excellent, its training and maintenance superb. But for reasons which will be shown, this marvelous weapon has been unable to stay with its foes in the long race of battle.

First Test Flunked

The conquests of Poland, France and the smaller European countries were mere exercises for the GAF. It came up to the Battle of Britain in full strength, confident in its ability to destroy the RAF (first step in the invasion of England, according to the Schlieffen Plan). Its estimates of the RAF fighter strength are believed to have been accurate. Consequently, it was a logical deduction that this puny force could be overrun rapidly by a series of devastating blows at the fighter fields of England.

The Plan began to roll on 8 August 1940. Day after day increasingly large formations of bombers sailed across the channel, and day after day many of them were knocked down. Despite their small numbers and small but steady losses, the British fighters seemed always to be in the sky at the right place, waiting. German Intelligence began to wonder if it had correctly estimated the size of the RAF Fighter Command. It had, but it did not know that an unknown weapon, familiar now but revolutionary then, was working on the side of the British. This was radar, which made possible the most economical deployment of British fighters. Also, the first of the GAF's few but incredibly costly mistakes revealed itself at this time. The German fighters and bombers both suffered from an insufficiency of armor and armament. And they did not have self-sealing fuel tanks.

The Schlieffen Plan was sputtering. An all-out effort was made to put it back on schedule. On 15 September every available bomber was employed against England. During the day, 185 enemy aircraft crashed on English soil. It is estimated that two or three times that number fell into the

sea, or on the continent. That ended the invasion. The Hun, seeing his forces disintegrating against an enemy fortress which was outwardly as strong as ever, switched to night attacks against British cities. That was his second mistake. He didn't realize how pitifully few Spits and Hurricanes there were left. British analysts have since estimated that the Fighter Command could not have held out for more than a few weeks more if the attacks had continued. The far-reaching consequences, had this error not been committed, are chilling to contemplate. England would have been invaded promptly, probably successfully, and the combined bomber offensive, on which the Allies subsequently pinned their hopes, and which was later to shake Germany to her foundations, might never have been launched.

Drawing on a large accumulated reserve, the GAF quickly recovered its losses. By the spring of 1941 it was more powerful than ever. But the RAF had doubled in the same period despite the German bombing attacks of the winter, and the golden opportunity was gone. Germany turned her attention toward Russia, having decisively lost the first real test of her air force. However, she had learned three lessons. Her planes, from now on, carried self-sealing tanks, more armor plate, and heavier offensive and defensive armament. With improved engines, they constituted an increasingly dangerous weapon.

Its Planes and Its Peculiarities

What was the nature of this weapon? It had, and still has, four outstanding characteristics. First, it concentrated on a very few types. It had one principal single-engine fighter, the Me-109E; one long-range fighter, the Me-110; one dive bomber, the Ju-87; three long-range bombers, the He-111, Do-17Z and Ju-88; one four-engine reconnaissance bomber, the FW-200K; and one outstanding transport, the Ju-52. Eight planes in all, compared to 17 which the USAAF has in large-scale operation today. There were other types including numerous small transports, flying boats, gliders, etc., but nine-tenths of the work of the GAF was done by the planes mentioned.

Second, these aircraft had to be versatile. In addition to doing their own jobs well they were expected to do numerous others. The Me-109, for example, has seen service as a day fighter, dive bomber, night fighter and photo plane; the Ju-88 as night fighter, day and night bomber, intruder and reconnaissance plane.

Continued on next page

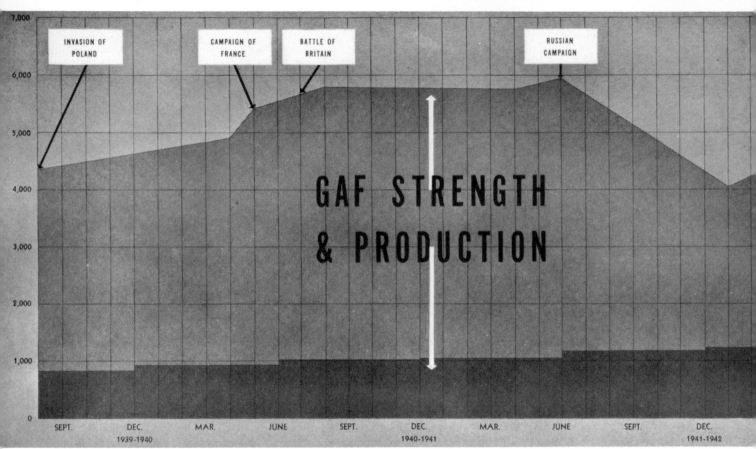

INVASION OF
POLAND

CAMPAIGN OF
FRANCE

BATTLE OF
BRITAIN

RUSSIAN
CAMPAIGN

GAF STRENGTH
& PRODUCTION

SEPT.   DEC.   MAR.   JUNE   SEPT.   DEC.   MAR.   JUNE   SEPT.   DEC.
1939-1940   1940-1941   1941-1942

Changes in GAF strength (medium tone) and production (dark tone) are shown above. Figures at left of graph

✠ GAF continued Third, progress has been measured by improvement of existing types and existing engines rather than by introduction of new ones. With the exception of two fighters, the FW-190 and Me-410, and the jet aircraft just now coming in, the GAF is still basically represented by the planes with which it started the war. The Me-109 now exists in the F and G models. An improved Me-110 is still in use. The Do-17Z has been improved and is now the Do-217, the Ju-88 has become the Ju-188. The Ju-87 is now a better Ju-87D. The He-111 is still itself.

Fourth, and in apparent contradiction to the third characteristic just mentioned, the GAF reflects a German tradition for bold and vigorous experimentation. This has persisted for five years despite the handicaps and shortages of the war, and the failure of some critical models to get into production. The great achievements of this tradition have been the introduction of the Me-163, the Me-262, the V-1 and the V-2, which represent the successful application of three new and different methods of aerial propulsion. To offset these successes, the German failure to develop a "heavy" bomber always rises to haunt them. Their so-called heavies are mediums by our standards. The only four-engine bomber they had was the FW-200K, a converted peace-time transport. It did its job, but only just. The He-177 was to replace it, but has never emerged in any quantity. Endless production problems and numerous bugs, apparently growing out of its unusual adaptation of four engines to only two propellers, have slowed it up. However, it has been just good enough to discourage abandoning it and starting something else. There are also others on which much time has been spent, and which have failed to pay off. Item: the He-280, a jet plane very much like the Me-262,

started at the same time but still developmental. Item: the He-113, a very small, very fast fighter modeled after a successful racing plane. It died almost at birth. Item: the Hs-129, a bullet-headed ground attack plane, slow and unwieldy. Item: the Me-321, largest glider in the world, capable of carrying 130 men and with a wing span forty feet greater than that of the B-29. Item: the pressurized Ju-86P, a high-altitude reconnaissance bomber. It flew so high in Africa that standard Spits couldn't get up to it, but something was wrong and it faded. There are others, some undoubtedly that Allied Intelligence doesn't even know about. But the experimenting goes on. In some instances, it is unrealistic to a degree. Although the GAF Bomber Command is now virtually defunct (as will be discussed shortly), this has not prevented continued work being done on at least six multi-engine bombers, despite the inescapable conclusion that none of them can expect to become operational in sufficient numbers in time to affect the outcome of the war.

The Third Error

To get back to the Battle of Britain, it continued with a series of shattering night blows at British cities, aimed at industry and morale, but these dwindled as British flak and night fighters contributed to the growing German conviction that the GAF was not winning the war with bombardment. This conviction was to have repercussions of the utmost seriousness. It lulled the Germans into a sense of security. If their magnificent air force had failed to destroy the small, weak, crowded target of England, how could anybody expect to do the same to a powerful and militant Germany, whose industry was scattered over an area many times the size of England, and much of it so far distant from England that it was believed that no bomber formation could reach

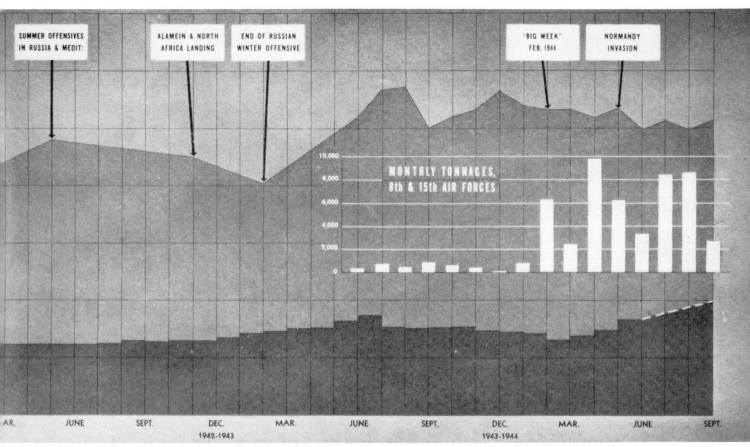

MONTHLY TONNAGES, 8th & 15th AIR FORCES

10,000
8,000
6,000
4,000
2,000
0

AR.   JUNE   SEPT.   DEC. 1942-1943   MAR.   JUNE   SEPT.   DEC. 1943-1944   MAR.   JUNE   SEPT.

show numbers of aircraft. Dotted white line at right indicates recent rising production trend.

it and live, much less get home. Besides, Germany had now learned about radar, and had an efficient early-warning net of its own. Those who believed that tactical support of ground operations was air power's true function seemed to have a strong case. It was to be further strengthened. The Wehrmacht plunged into Russia, and much of the energy of the GAF became involved there. In addition, all available long-range aircraft were put to work over the Atlantic on anti-convoy work. In neither instance was high-level bombardment decisive.

This failure to reap any conclusive rewards from three applications of heavy bombardment can be traced directly to the initial German belief that an air force should be tactical. It prevented them from going deeply into the subject of strategic bombardment, which in turn affected their bomber design and even the size of their bomber force. It undoubtedly contributed to the slowness in getting the He-177 under way, and to the failure to develop a satisfactory substitute when the 177 began to emerge as a lemon. And it is easy to understand why no effort was made at abnormal enlargement of the bomber force after the Battle of Britain. You do not again put your shirt on a horse after it fails to come home the first time. Nor was the fighter force abnormally expanded. It seemed big enough to support contemplated operations. It did not fear enemy air attacks.

At the outset of the war actual GAF strength in combat aircraft is believed to have been about 4,500 planes. This was backed by a reserve of 4,000. Production was a little under 1,000 a month. Losses during the Battle of Britain, the Norwegian campaign, and the invasion of Greece ate steadily into this reserve, which was whittled down to 1,500 planes at the start of the Russian campaign in June 1941. At the same time, actual strength had risen to 6,000 through

increasingly rapid movement of planes from reserves to operational units in order to meet expanding demands. During the next six months wastage in Russia cut reserves to 500 and actual strength to 4,000. For the first time since the start of the war all was not serene on the German military horizon. An immense effort to capture Moscow was failing, a British offensive was being launched in Africa, and RAF bombing attacks in western Germany were beginning to assume serious proportions. The GAF was smaller and weaker than at any time since the start of the war. It has been established that at some point in the first half of 1942 the decision was finally forced on the Germans to reorganize their aircraft industry and build it up. This called for increasing utilization of foreign workers (which by the end of 1943 comprised over 60 percent of the aircraft industry's personnel), a great simplification and standardization of jobs so that these foreign workers could be used, and the development of component and assembly "complexes" in order to achieve maximum output by centralizing production.

The Complex Has Its Day

To meet the growing threats of RAF attacks by night and USAAF attacks by day, the increase was to be entirely in single-engine and twin-engine fighters. Production of other types was not stepped up, and the shift over of the GAF from an offensive to a defensive role was made official by the steady curtailment of bomber production from this point on. This fundamental change in policy is best illustrated by the fact that production of single-engine fighters jumped 375 percent between January 1942 and October 1944, while production of long-range bombers declined 85 percent during the same period. Three Me-109 complexes were developed

Continued on next page

Fighter Kills

These 8th and 9th AF gun camera pictures represent the subtraction from the GAF of only 22 of its aircraft. Yet it is a bad day when our fighters fail to get many more. On 27 November, for example, an 8th AF fighter sweep garnered 98 for a loss of 11. The day before the bag was 114. Simple arithmetic of this kind helps explain why present monthly production of German fighters is insufficient to maintain the GAF as an effective weapon.

at Leipzig, Wiener Neustadt, and Regensburg; and four FW-190 complexes, whose facilities were centered at Kassel, Oschersleben, Tutow and Marienburg. Manufacture of the Me-110, 210 and 410 was at Brunswick, Gotha and Budapest.

Germany has been criticized for this centralizing of her aircraft industry. Such criticism is not warranted, even though the theory of centralization did spring from the false belief that the complexes would be safe from Allied bombers. Actually, it was the false belief itself which was dangerous because it had led Germany into a more fundamental error. If, after the Battle of Britain, she had realized that she had just two years before the blistering wind of the Combined Bomber Offensive would hit her, she would have started *then* to enlarge and centralize her aircraft industry. If she had done this, her complexes could have operated without serious interruption during that period and produced literally thousands of fighters. This would have resulted in much greater losses of Allied bombers when

their strategic attacks began, which would have meant a slower buildup of strength in the 8th AF and RAF Bomber Command, which in turn would have greatly reduced the damage they could have been doing. This would have prolonged the productive life of the complexes and added still further to the number of defensive fighters which the GAF would have had available. The Allies could not have shifted to the strategic oil campaign when they did, nor could they have launched an invasion when they did. With luck we probably would be at this moment where we were a year ago, still slugging at the aircraft complexes.

What actually happened was this: German plane production of all types had risen slowly from 850 a month in 1939 to 1,300 by the end of 1942. It was at this point that the fruits of centralization at Leipzig, Regensburg and Wiener Neustadt began to ripen. By July 1943 production was up to 1,740 a month, which is sufficient proof that the idea of the complex was a sound one if timed right. GAF actual

Continued on next page

Me-262, Germany's most successful jet plane, is nailed by 8th AF P-51.   *Another Me-262, caught between two*

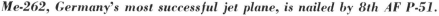

strength reflected this increase immediately, rising from 4,100 to 5,600 in the first six months of 1943. It would have continued to grow as the result of the program expansion (which called for monthly production of 2,900 by the end of 1944), but unfortunately for Germany, the 8th AF was now large enough to launch the first of a series of crippling blows at the complexes. Wiener Neustadt, Regensburg, Oschersleben, Kassel, Marienburg and Leipzig were all seriously damaged between July and September. It was during this period that the bloodiest air battles of the war were fought. Germany developed the airborne rocket, whose threat was only parried by our perfection of overlapping escort tactics and the final delivery of sufficient numbers of long-range fighters to accompany our heavies to almost any point in Europe. Because of heavy attrition, the GAF could only show an increase in strength of 300 aircraft during the bitterly contested latter half of 1943. But Allied bomber and fighter strength grew enormously. It uncorked a series of hammer blows at the complexes in February during a period of intensive operations now known as the "Big Week" and rightly regarded as one of the great achievements of American airpower.

Exit the Complex

By rights the GAF should have been crippled. That it was not is a tribute to the ingenuity and speed with which the complexes were dispersed. This went ahead so rapidly that even though April 1944 saw the largest tonnage in history dropped on enemy aircraft plants, their production actually rose. The following figures tell the story:

	February	March	April
Tonnage	6,372	2,412	9,846
Total production	1,400	1,300	1,400

In other words, the maximum effort of which Allied bombers were then capable, considering their other obligations, could not prevent a decentralized German aircraft industry from slowly increasing its production. This is a fact of the utmost importance, and it explains why tonnages against plane factories have declined since April. The general opinion that plane production had been wiped out, when the GAF failed to show up for the Normandy invasion, when it failed to oppose the Riviera landings or the rapid Allied ground advances during the Battle of France, is entirely erroneous. Production has, as a matter of plain fact, increased steadily since March, and is at present greater (in number of aircraft produced) than at any previous time. The total *weight* of aircraft produced, however, has not materially increased. It cannot, because Germany has now thrown into aircraft production all the resources and manpower she has available. As soon as the shift to making nothing but small planes is completed (one bomber equals two or three fighters in

8th AF P-51s, get same 50-cal. massage.   *Death of an Me-163 is recorded by gun camera of 8th Air Force P-47.*

weight, man hours and materials), there will be no further increase in the number of aircraft produced monthly. What is more probable, it will tend to drop, as the growing strains of a losing war begin to exact a heavier and heavier toll from the over-all German economy.

Recent Allied attacks have been aimed at engine plants, where dispersion is most difficult, at air parks where planes are stored, at jet production centers, and at those component and assembly plants which appear large and active enough to warrant attacks. The difficulty of the Allied task in further reducing German plane production by bombing is indicated by the fact that there are now more than 200 known places where some form of aircraft production or assembly takes place, plus a somewhat smaller number where it is reported, but where the nature of the construction or the location of the plant is not confirmed. Also, as has often been rumored in the past, production has now in some cases gone underground.

Where, then, is the GAF? In a sentence, it is snowed under. It can only run the risk of large-scale opposition to our bombardment missions when, through our failure to effect rendezvous, it sees an opportunity for an attack, or when our target is so important that it feels compelled to rise in defense regardless of the consequences. Its repair and maintenance facilities are strained, so is its manpower. It suffers from a shortage of well-equipped fields, the best of

which were in France. And, most important, it is very short of fuel, which has seriously curtailed its training program; all contributing to its present low degree of fighting value.

Too Little Too Late

That is the situation as it exists now. The GAF is larger than it was in 1939. Its planes are better. But it is virtually impotent because of the omnipotence of the air power opposing it. On two successive days late in November 1944 it flew 800 and 750 sorties, the largest defensive GAF effort of the war. But operations of this kind are inconclusive. They do not stop Allied attacks, and have lately resulted in losses to the GAF on the order of 100 fighters at a time. Its offensive capabilities are at an even lower ebb, having virtually vanished as one bomber unit after another has become inactive. The V-1 and V-2 programs, which in essence are attempts to substitute a cheap and expendable bomber force for the one thus being cannibalized, are brilliant engineering achievements, but both came "too little and too late" to affect anything but the peace. The jet program, also a brilliant achievement, is likewise too little and too late. Its relation to the present situation is best expressed by the flier who said he would prefer to fight a war with 100 P-36s flown by well-trained pilots than with 10 P-51s flown by half-baked pilots. In the air over Europe numbers and well-trained crews reign supreme. And we have both.

Continued on next page

Continued on next page

Confidential

Underground assembly of FW-190s was started in France when bombing of facilities at Merignac (above) persuaded Germans to move to large cave at Astier.

Entrance of cave at Astier (65 miles east of Bordeaux) is shown above. Originally a

Cluster of German and American lathes was brought to Astier from above-ground plants at Merignac, Bacalan, Degles.

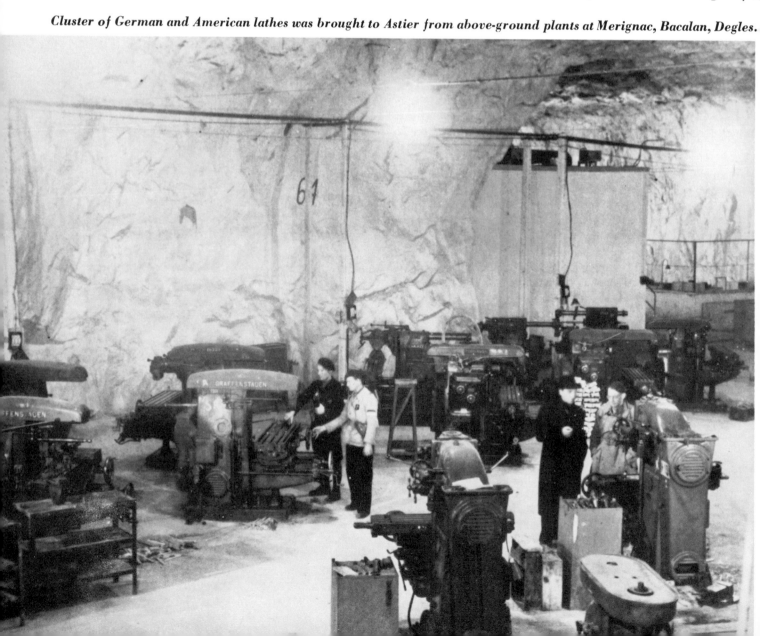

limestone quarry, it has 500,000 square feet of floor space, extends 1,500 feet into hillside.

FW-190 fuselages are stacked along wall, waiting patiently but hopelessly to be assembled. Cave has its own power and light plant, also a lake 75 feet deep.

Underground dining room, with modern kitchen behind balcony in background, can feed all Astier's workmen.

ETO ESCORT

Three-Dimensional Diagrams Show Route and Escort Formations Evolved After Two Years of Rugged Battling with the Hun

When American heavies began bombing Europe in the summer of 1942, they sometimes had the benefit of diversionary sweeps by RAF fighters; more often they were on their own. They never had escort as we know it today. This was not dangerous at first because of the tentative nature of German fighter attacks and the shallowness of our penetrations. But it soon became so. As our formations grew, increasing numbers of defensive fighters were massed in the lowlands to match that growth. Attempts were made to overwhelm us by mass attacks of several hundred Me-109s and FW-190s. Later, rocket-carrying Me-110s and 410s were thrown into the struggle. The need for escort fighters became critical.

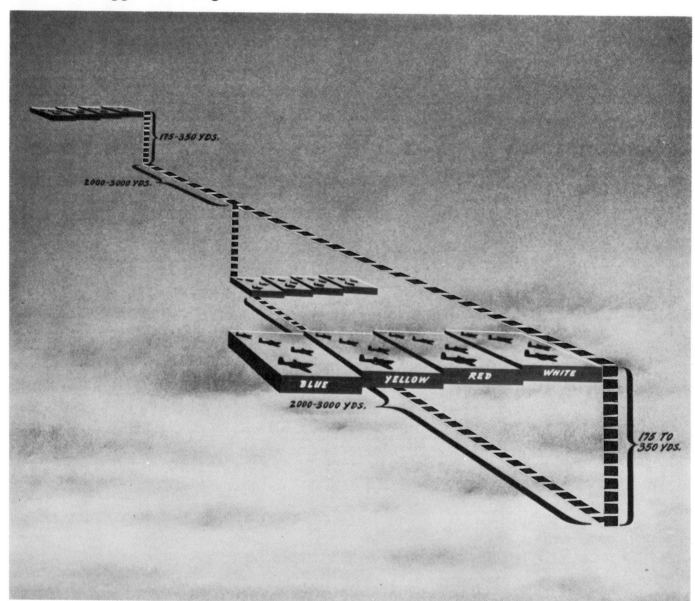

CLIMB FORMATION. A year ago, 8th AF fighter groups headed for the Continent with a medium power setting in climb and cruise, in order to obtain an altitude of 25,000-27,000 feet before crossing the enemy coast, and to be above the bombers at rendezvous. With the Hun moving inland, fighter groups can now climb from base to rendezvous at minimum power settings, thus extending their endurance.

The formation flown is a flat one, its purpose being to have units flying parallel to and opposite each other to cover each others' blind spots. Distances between squadrons are given above, each squadron flying a close formation of flights staggered down in trail, 300 yards apart. Flying as close as shown is particularly effective against large numbers of enemy aircraft, as it allows most of the group to engage.

First to reach England in the spring of 1943 were three P-47 groups. On 4 May they received their baptism, immediately proving themselves. They successfully shepherded 79 heavies to Antwerp and back without loss, whereas an unescorted force three days before had lost seven out of 78 during a mission to St. Nazaire. These early P-47s operated without belly tanks. The Hun soon learned their range, and waited to attack the bombers after their escort had turned for home. On 28 July a rude shock was delivered with the introduction of a 75-gallon belly tank which increased the range of the P-47 to 280 miles. By the time he had adjusted himself to this novelty the Hun found himself coping with a 108-gallon tank which further extended P-47

range to 320 miles. During the summer and fall four more P-47 groups were made operational. In October P-38s appeared, and in December the first of a swarm of P-51s, which were eventually to provide continuous cover on missions of 600 miles or more. There were now no open spaces where German fighters could gang up. In the encounters following the P-51's introduction, the enemy suffered heavily, lapsing finally into a practice of attacking the bombers only when the fighter escort had failed to effect rendezvous.

Our fighters now play an offensive role. They engage the enemy and destroy him wherever possible, in contrast to their earlier, primarily protective function.

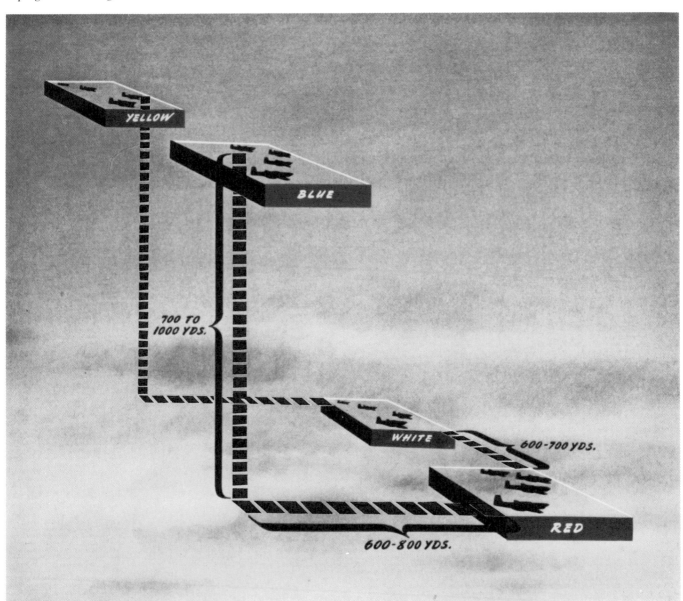

BATTLE FORMATION. Upon crossing into enemy territory, the tight group formation shown opposite is loosened somewhat, and each squadron assumes the pattern shown above. Red and blue flights move off to the right 600-800 yards. Blue and yellow flights fly parallel to one another and behind and above white and red to give them cover. If the squadron is alone, these high flights are placed 700-1,000 yards up. If it is in a group, they are placed only 175-350 yards up. Too much spreading at this point is dangerous. The leader has a hard time controlling his squadrons, identification of all elements as friendly aircraft is not always possible, and excessive power must be used by pilots in order to maintain formation in turns. Also, in case of attack, only one or two flights can engage the enemy.

Continued on next page

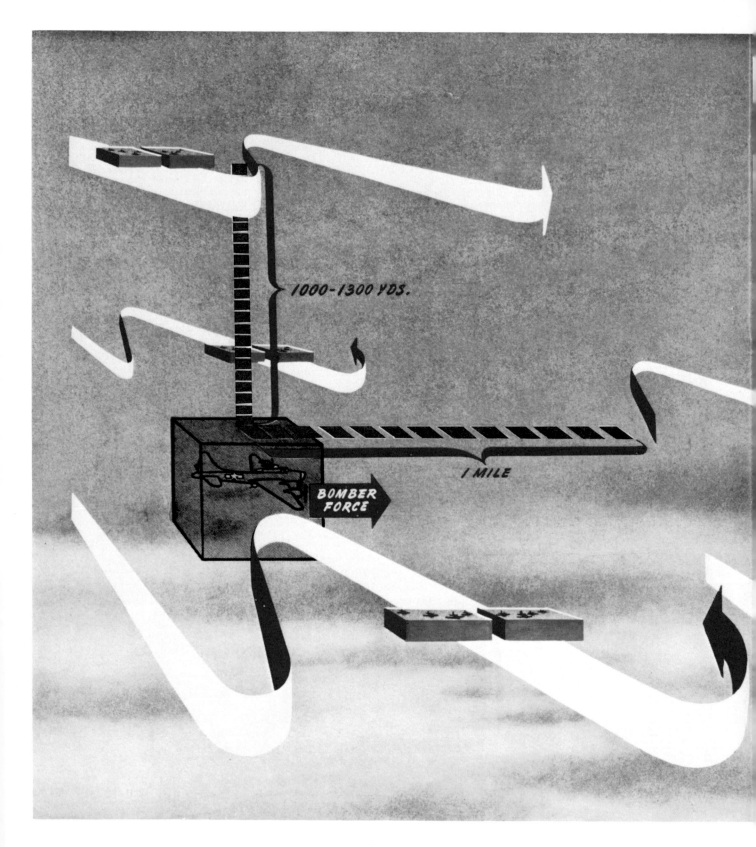

ESCORT FORMATION. The above diagram shows the most common 8th AF deployment of a fighter group around a bomber force after rendezvous has been effected. One squadron is flying a mile in front of the bombers. It is divided into sections of eight planes each (two flights), one level with the bombers, one slightly higher. Their mission is to roam out ahead and to each side of their big friends in the hope of sighting enemy fighters which may be waiting in ambush. They weave constantly, and because of this their flights may fly in trail as well as side by side as shown above. The second squadron is flying just the same as the first, but with one flight on each side of the bombers instead of a mile ahead.

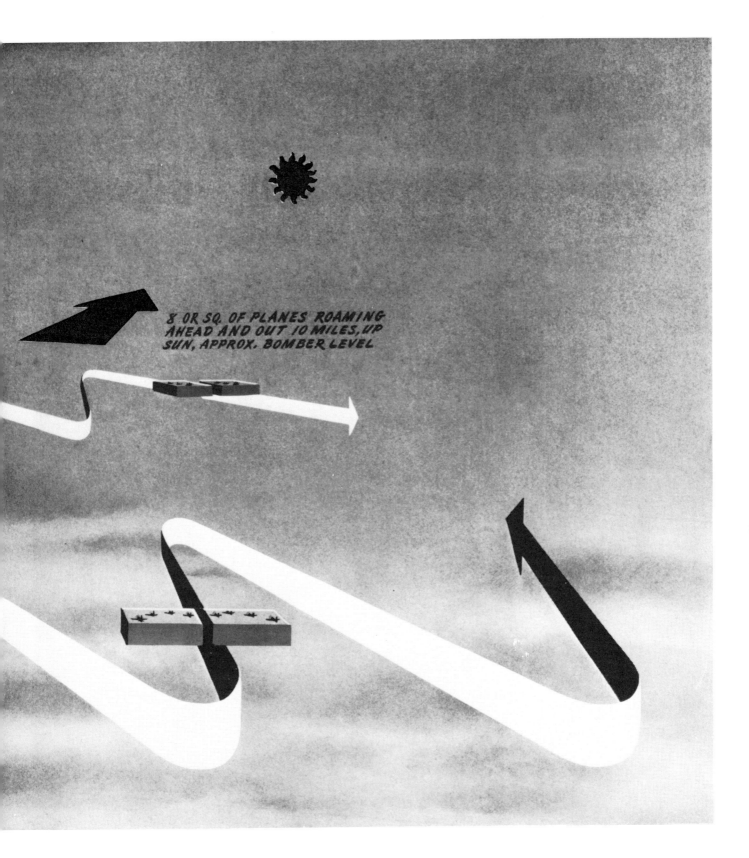

8 OR SQ. OF PLANES ROAMING
AHEAD AND OUT 10 MILES, UP
SUN, APPROX. BOMBER LEVEL

They may even lag a little behind to be prepared for enemy formations ganging up above and to the rear. The third squadron is also split. Half of it flies top cover, roaming 1,000-1,300 yards above the bombers. The other half flies about ten miles ahead and up sun, to intercept any bandits who may be queuing up and who will be invisible at that distance to the rest of the escort because of the bright sun.

All these planes play an aggressive role. They are expected to pursue and destroy any enemy aircraft approaching, even if it means leaving the bombers unprotected. However, the leader must exercise discretion, and should not commit all his planes to attack a small decoy force.

Continued on next page

High fighter cover passes over bombers after rendezvous. They have flown course parallel to or slightly converging with that of bombers, can spot big formations 15-25 miles away. Note nearly invisible bombers on cloud horizon.

Single flight of high cover weaves above bomber box. Thick persistent contrails like these simplify rendezvous problem considerably, make bombers visible for 30 miles or more. This flight is showing tendency to get too widely spread to afford good protection, may not be able to work as a unit in case of sudden enemy attack from above.

From underneath, a flight of high-cover P-51s looks like this. Contrails clearly show constant weaving that enables individual pilots to cover each others' blind spots. Flight leader is probably second from left. His wingman has just crossed over behind him. Second element has also crossed over from left to right, will soon swing back into position.

Tremendous concentration of continuously pointed heavy flak rises to meet 15th AF Libs over Vienna.

GERMAN FLAK

It is More Rugged Than Ever

To offset the declining effectiveness of the GAF in the air, the flak defenses of vital German targets are growing in density every week. Recent ETO figures show 62 percent of definitely allocated heavy bomber combat losses result from flak, 38 percent from fighters. Enormous concentrations of AA now exist around Leipzig and Merseburg, matching those already existing in the Ruhr Valley and in the neighborhood of Vienna (above).

Over Munich, during attack on rail yard, B-24 from the 15th AF is turned into a torch by hit from heavy AA shell.

Seconds later, right wing of B-24, shorn off by intense fire in root, follows rest of aircraft in last flaming plunge.

BUT WORK GOES ON
8th Gets in Greatest Blows

Like an industrial complex, which originates in the automobile business and then spreads out to include such fields as radio, refrigerators and diesel locomotives, is the 8th Air Force, always ready and willing to get into a new business. In September it undertook to fly in supplies at 200 feet to the airborne armies in Holland. In October it dried up a canal (below). In November it dropped 5,000 tons of frags on enemy front line positions in one day. At the same time it has never lost sight of its primary mission: to numb German industry (see next 6 pages).

And the blows get heavier. In October 17,717 bombers dropped 43,615 tons on German industrial targets.

Smoke markers and GP head for Mitteland Canal through overcast.

Mitteland Canal after 8th AF PFF attack on 26 Oct. Five barges were washed through 80-ft. breach in embankment cut by 851-ton load. Canal and adjacent aqueduct were both drained. More barges are seen stranded on canal bottom.

BARGES
WASHED OUT THRU GAP

FLOOD WATER FROM BREA
PARTIALLY BLOCKED WESE
WITH SILT

NEAR MISSES

85 FT. GAP

Continued on next page

AERO ENGINE PLANT HIT
DB Works at Gaggenau Reduced to Shambles

Because of the elaborate plant setup required to manufacture aircraft engines, their production cannot be dispersed as readily as can that of other aircraft components. This explains why, even as late as the autumn of 1944, there still remained in Germany juicy targets like the Gaggenau Daimler Benz plant shown here. After two attacks in less than a month, Gaggenau is now, nearly three months later, still in bad shape. Lately repairs have been started on the huge areas of roofing which have been blown off. Piles of debris have been carted away, or pathways cleared between them. But latest reconnaissance indicates that Gaggenau will not be completely operational for some time.

Gaggenau before. Plant is a large one located on a bend in the river near Baden Baden. It produces motor vehicles as well as DB aircraft engines for Me-109s and Me-110s.

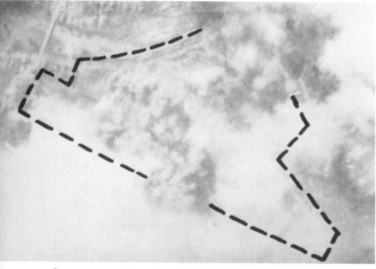

Gaggenau during. Previously damaged by 8th AF bombers on 10 September, plant is seen at height of second blow on 3 Oct. Bulk of 403 tons fell squarely on the target.

Gaggenau after. Damage is extremely heavy throughout plant. All main buildings have been hit, most of them nearly demolished. Photo cover as late as 27 November shows only

52   **Confidential**

minor clearance and reconstruction. Annotated are: (1) final assembly and machine shop gutted, (2) large machine shops very badly damaged with much of roof destroyed, (3) stamp-ing, pressing and heat treating shops badly damaged, (4) body assembly and paint shops nearly destroyed, (5) wood-working shop half gutted, (6) power station inactive.

Continued on next page

Attack on Hamburg/Glinde on 6 October nearly destroyed its three main ordnance buildings (1), did serious

ORDNANCE DEPOT ROCKED
No Business As Usual During Alterations

Caught in the relentless spotlight of this superb damage photograph, Hamburg/Glinde ordnance depot resembles nothing so much as an ant colony under a log—with the log removed. Like eggs piled hastily to one side are the enormous stacks of supplies visible at the left and top of

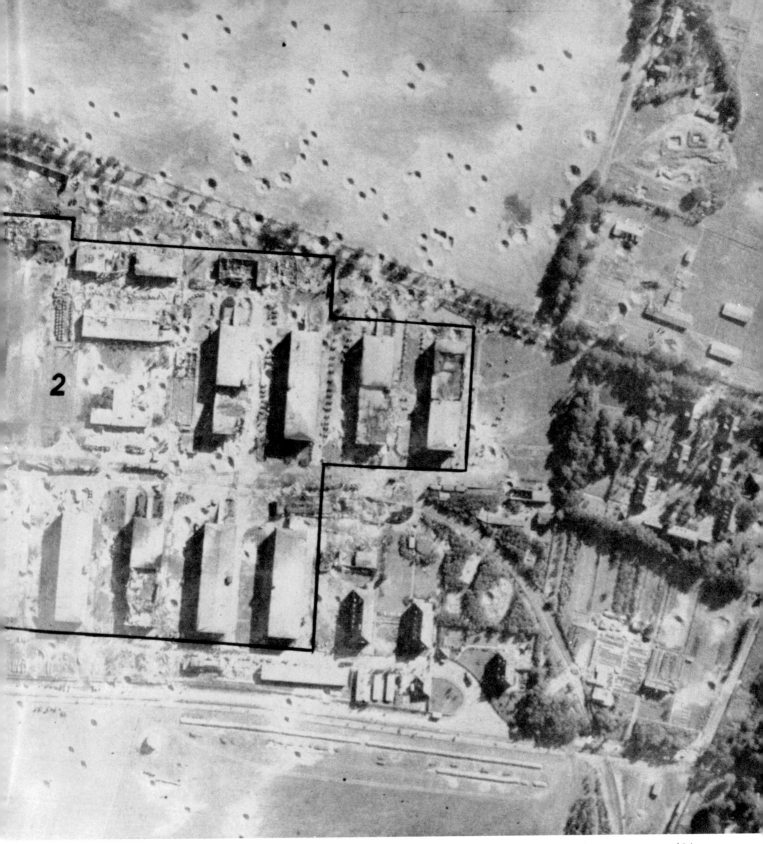

damage to three of twelve standard ramped buildings (2), destroyed smaller unidentified building (3).

the picture. Like ants themselves are the numerous trucks and freight cars. Like the ruptured galleries and storerooms of the anthill are the roofless warehouses, their contents open to the sun and sky.

The attack on Hamburg/Glinde was made on 6 October by the relatively small force of 89 bombers, which crossed the target from Southwest to Northeast, straddling it perfectly with 637 500-lb. GP and 319 100-lb. IB. Of the three largest warehouses, one was almost completely demolished, one two-thirds destroyed, one half destroyed.

Continued on next page

SYNTHETIC OIL
Two Huge Plants Walloped

Misburg before. Synethetic plant with monthly pre-attack capacity of 25,000 tons looked like this in 1942.

Bottrop before. This synthetic oil plant is located near Gelsenkirchen in the heart of the Ruhr, had a monthly pre-attack capacity of 8,000 metric tons. Photo was taken after plant had suffered some damage in earlier attacks, but before 19 November mission.

Misburg smolders after attack of 29 November by 391 8th AF heavy bombers who dropped 1,152 tons of 500-lb. GP. Wreckage is widespread and includes damage to the following: (1) lubricating oil treatment plant, (2) boiler house and transformer, (3) distillation, (4) de-asphalting plant, (5) tankage, (6) distillation and polymerization units, (7) Dubbs cracking unit. Misburg was attacked nine times in 1944, most successfully on 20 June and 12 September. Present capacity is estimated to be down to about 15,000 metric tons a month.

Bottrop after. Plant looked like this after series of 8th AF attacks, the latest one on 19 November. Annotated are: (1) cooling towers wrecked, (2) tankage about one-third destroyed, (3) three direct hits on group of tanks camouflaged as slag heap, (4) boiler house, power plant and transformer station heavily damaged, (5) injector houses and hydrogenation stalls moderately damaged, (6) distillation units undamaged, (7) solvent regeneration plant slightly damaged, (8) coal crushing plant, colliery buildings and headgear slightly damaged. Numerous small unidentified buildings are damaged or destroyed. Dotted lines show location of camouflage, much of it still visible in photo, although badly tattered. Originally it covered all the tankage in the western and northern parts of plant.

ⓞbituary

Above is a recent portrait of the late but unlamented Jap island of Jaluit, which died after a lingering illness brought about by an overdose of 7th AF bombs. The deceased was known in its brief heyday as an "unsinkable carrier" for Jap planes in the Marshalls. From November 1943 through September 1944, Jaluit was blasted by approximately 1,500 tons dropped by B-24s of the 7th AF. These attacks tapered off sharply after May 1944, with the last reported mission being on 21 September when three B-24s dropped three tons for old time's sake.

Though officially dead, the corpse still gets up occasionally and rattles its bones, whereupon it is smacked down again by Navy and Marine light bombers and fighters, which have taken over the job since 1 October. They have made about 1,000 sorties and 35 strikes, using Jaluit for practice operations as if it were a corpse in a medical school.